AF352614

Convergence amidst Difference

SUNY Series in the Philosophy of the Social Sciences

Lenore Langsdorf, editor

CONVERGENCE AMIDST DIFFERENCE

Philosophical Conversations Across National Boundaries

Calvin O. Schrag

STATE UNIVERSITY OF NEW YORK PRESS

Published by
State University of New York Press, Albany

For information, address State University of New York Press,
90 State Street, Suite 700, Albany, NY 12207

Production by Christine L. Hamel
Marketing by Susan Petrie

Library of Congress Cataloging-in-Publication Data

Schrag, Calvin O.
   Convergence amidst difference : philosophical conversations across national boundaries /
by Calvin O. Schrag.
      p. cm. — (SUNY series in the philosophy of the social sciences)
   Includes bibliographical references and index.
   ISBN 0-7914-6203-X (alk. paper)
   1. Philosophy, Modern—20th century. I. Title. II. Series.

B804.S375 2004
190'.9'0511—dc22

                                                                                        2004041704

PREVIOUS PUBLICATIONS BY AUTHOR

Existence and Freedom: Towards an Ontology of Human Finitude (1961)

Experience and Being: Prolegomena to a Future Ontology (1969)

Radical Reflection and the Origin of the Human Sciences (1980)

Communicative Praxis and the Space of Subjectivity (1986)

The Resources of Rationality: A Response to the Postmodern Challenge (1992)

Philosophical Papers: Betwixt and Between (1994)

The Self after Postmodernity (1997)

God as Otherwise than Being: Toward a Semantics of the Gift (2002)

CONTENTS

PREFACE

THE FIVE ESSAYS that make up the format of the following philosophical explorations provide an account of a philosophical journey along a path from a hermeneutic of sense and reference to a transfigured concept of the subject and a delimited metaphysics to a new notion of rationality. This new notion of rationality has been named *transversal* rationality and is recommended as a reliable resource in defining the task of philosophy for the future. The journey unfolds as a transnational itinerary that moves across the terrain of five different countries on which a thematic development is forged through conversations across national boundaries on the related issues at stake. In its progression, marking out a time period of more than a decade, an effort has been made to work out strategies of transcultural communication, drawing upon the philosophical contributions in each of the represented countries, striving for a mutual understanding that is fashioned both *in spite of* and *because of* differences. As a continuing experiment in communicating across differing perspectives on the topics at issue, the envisioned goal of the project is that of opening up new directions for a possible *post*-national philosophical understanding.

The essay *Traces of Meaning and Reference: From Epistemology to Linguistics to Hermeneutics* has its origins in a presentation and discussion that took place at Druzba, Bulgaria, in September 1988 under the auspices of the Bulgarian Academy of Sciences. This was at a time when an iron curtain mentality was still prevalent within the Bulgarian academies of higher learning. Dialectical materialism was the dominant philosophical persuasion in many of the universities of the land. However, insofar as the sponsored conference "Models of Meaning" was specifically focused on linguistics and semantic theory an opportunity was opened up to address issues against the backdrop of a wider perspective of the Eastern European cultural heritage. It was thus that I chose to initiate the conversation by proceeding not from the contributions of a Marx or a Lenin but rather from the legacy of Mikhail M. Bakhtin. More specifically, my intention was to illustrate how meaning and reference live and move about within a Bakhtinian chronotope of assimilated historical time and space. (An earlier draft of the Bulgaria lecture has been published in *Current Advances in Semantic Theory*, edited by Maxim Stamenov, John Benjamins Publishing Company: Philadelphia, 1992, under the title "Traces of Meaning and Reference: Phenomenological and Hermeneutical Explorations").

The second essay, *The Subject in Question and the Question about the Questioner,* developed out of a symposium presentation and discussion at Oxford University in March 1993. It was during the early part of the decade of the 1990s that talk about the demise of the subject was very much in the philosophical news of the day. My presentation was designed as a response to this philosophical situation of the time. Plainly enough, the news about the passing of the subject in the varied reports about its death/dissolution/deconstruction came principally from across the channel. It was thus that I felt a sense of urgency to remind my British interlocutors about a contribution bearing on the topic by one of their more illustrious twentieth-century philosophers, Gilbert Ryle. I asked them to recall Ryle's surprisingly favorable comments on Martin Heidegger's *Sein und Zeit,* even though admittedly he remained quite critical of Heidegger's conclusions in this work. Ryle's review of Heidegger's *Sein und Zeit* work appeared in 1929 in the philosophy journal *Mind* just two years after the book was published. This was the first major review of the work in the English-speaking world. In his review Ryle extols Heidegger as a philosopher who "shows himself to be a thinker of real importance by the immense subtlety and searchingness of his examination of consciousness," and then goes on to provide the reader with one of the earliest and most succinct definitions of Heidegger's project of deconstruction, to wit: the requirement "to think beyond the stock categories of orthodox philosophy and psychology" (*Mind: A Quarterly Review of Psychology and Philosophy,* vol. 38, 1929, p. 370). Forty years later Ryle fashioned his own project of deconstruction in *The Concept of Mind* (New York: Barnes and Noble, 1949) by dismantling the Cartesian invention of the mind as a ghost in a machine, and by doing so he raised some unsettling questions about the destiny of the concept of the subject for all future philosophical investigations.

Addressing my British colleagues in a country whose principal contribution was the inauguration of philosophical empiricism, I deemed it appropriate to recall for them some of the resources in William James's *radical* empiricism, suggesting how James's idiosyncratic empiricist turn could be of help in identifying the subject who is in question. The hallmark of the radical empiricism as proposed by William James was its accent on the holisitic configuration of what he came to call "the world experienced." This emphasis on holism and contextuality provided a sheet-anchor against tendencies toward an *abstract* empiricism that pulverized experience into decontextualized and discrete granular sense impressions. In calling our attention to the contextualized background of our perception, our discourse, and our action, James opened up a vibrant space for a reclamation of the subject in question.

The essay *The Recovery of the Phenomenological Subject* continues the discussion of the fate of the subject that was broached in the Oxford symposium. The topic remains basically the same, but the interlocutors are different, selected from the French scene of later twentieth-century continental thought. It was thus that the original version bore the subtitle "In Conversation with Derrida, Ricoeur, and Levinas." The format of the lecture shapes up as a project of reclaiming certain resources in the phenomenological tradition, and particularly in its French developments, for addressing the issue of the whereabouts of the subject in the current philosophical state of affairs.

In my conversation with Derrida, I am quick to express my appreciation for the insights that he has provided in his deconstruction of the subject as metaphysical substrate and epistemological zero-point origin. My critical concerns have to do principally with the delimitations that travel with the project of deconstruction, culminating in a realization that the truth of deconstruction resides in a recognition that no complete deconstruction is possible. The identification of the "who" involved in the deconstruction is a requirement that seems to return time and again, inviting a reexamination of the phenomenological notion of the *Lebenswelt* as a possible site for the self-knowledge and self-constitution of the subject. Levinas does well to point out the limitations of Husserl's celebrated phenomenological reduction of consciousness designed to yield a stable transcendental ego.

Yet, we are not ready to abandon all phenomenological resources. Circumventing the protocols of an ego-based transcendental phenomenology we propose instead a nonegological phenomenological investigation that would explore the space on the hither side of the modern transcendental-empirical doublet. Our critical conversation with Ricouer turns specifically on the resources of narrative in a project of recovering the phenomenological subject. (A French version of the essay, *La récupération du suject phénoménologique,* was published in *Analecta Husserliana,* ed. A-T Tymieniecka, Kluwer Academic Publishers, 1997.)

The fourth essay was initially presented in Saint Petersburg at the invitation of the Saint Petersburg Branch of the Russian Academy of Sciences in October 1997 on the occasion of the annual meeting of the revitalized Russian Metaphysical Society. Duly concerned about the effects of postmodernism on the traditional discipline of metaphysics, members of the Russian Society sensed a widespread loss of nerve on matters metaphysical among the proponents of postmodernism within certain philosophical enclaves in Western Europe and the United States. If postmodernism marks the end of metanarratives, and if metaphysics is but yet another metanarrative among others, whither the metaphysics of the future? This was the question and concern that informed and invigorated the discussions at the University of Saint Petersburg.

In my address to the Russian Academy, I found it appropriate to recall the contributions to the topic of the conference by one of Russia's most illustrious cultural icons, Fyodor Michailovitch Dostoevsky. I reminded my interlocutors that it was none other than their own Nicholas Berdyaev who referred to Dostoevsky as "Russia's greatest metaphysician." With Dostoevsky's profound grasp of the fragility of the human condition in the background, I made an effort to respond to the challenge of postmodernism and its skepticism on matters metaphysical by drafting a minimalist metaphysics rooted in an ontology of human finitude.

The last essay, *The Task of Philosophy for the New Millennium,* was presented in its initial format at Charles University in March 2000 at the invitation of the Academy of Sciences of the Czech Republic. The topic of the essay was selected in commemoration of Edmund Husserl's famous Prague lectures sixty-five years earlier, in which he broached a similar line of inquiry. The Prague lectures that

Husserl presented in 1935 under the title "The Crisis of European Sciences and Psychology" formed the basis for his celebrated volume, *The Crisis of European Sciences and Transcendental Phenomenology,* posthumously published under the editorship of Walter Biemel in 1954. This later work by Husserl continues to stand as one of the most brilliant and profound envisionments of the future task of philosophy from the vantage point of mid-twentieth-century philosophical developments.

My Prague presentation, in the distant shadows of Husserl's masterful accomplishment, was an attempt at readdressing the issues that he raised in regard to the resources of rationality. This is clearly a task that needs to be undertaken time and again, and it is a task that is particularly urgent when the call for reason is muted by societal forces of unreason. The central thesis in the following lecture turns on a delineation of a refiguration of reason as *transversal* in character, effecting a passage between the Scylla of hegemonic claims for universality and the Charybdis of an anarchic particularity. (An abbreviated version of the originally presented essay has appeared in a Czech translation, *Filosofie ve Školnich Lavicích: Úkol filsosfie v novém tisícileti,* in the Czech philosophy journal *FILOSOFICKÝ ČASOPIS,* Ročnik 48, 2000, čislo 4. The current essay is expanded both in its format and development of issues as compared with the initial presentation).

The consolidation of themes displayed in the five essays reduces to an assessment of the fortunes of philosophical discourse on the related issues of interpretive understanding, the role of the subject in the history of self-formation, the dynamics of transversality, and the fate of metaphysics at the turn of the twenty-first century. Emerging from struggles for communication contextualized in concrete situations of speaker/interlocutor exchange, situated in the midst of cultural differences on the philosophical task, the essays are oriented toward a more general readership. The emerging proposals and reflections have been shaped through the dialogic interactions with the hearers of the public presentations. It is thus that the current project is basically an exercise in philosophical rhetoric and communication across national divides. The technical apparatus of the usual philosophical discourse has been recast for a wider public and scholarly footnotes have been kept at a minimum.

WEST LAFAYETTE, INDIANA, APRIL 2003

ESSAY I

Traces of Meaning and Reference

From Epistemology to Linguistics to Hermeneutics

THE EPISTEMOLOGICAL PROBLEMATIC

A PECULIAR TRAIT of modern philosophy has been its obsession with the problems of meaning and reference. These intertwined problems became prominently inscribed in the annals of philosophical discourse as a result of the epistemological turn maneuvered by Descartes. With his invention of the mind as a translucent ego-cogito, whose principal function it was to provide accurate representations of reality, Descartes placed upon the quests for meaning and reference some rather staggering demands. The ego-cogito was shouldered with the formidable task of determining meaning through the instrumentation of clear and distinct ideas and delivering reference via a route of trustworthy inferences. It was in this manner that the problems of meaning and reference came to be defined against the backdrop of the modern theoretico-epistemological paradigm.

The repeated attempts to solve these twin problems in the history of continental rationalism (from Descartes to Husserl) and in the history of British empiricism (from Locke to Russell) continued to proceed within the parameters set by the epistemological paradigm. Some of these efforts were boldly metaphysical in design; others had recourse to a variety of reductionisms, either of a psychological or logical sort. The story of the manifold vagaries that travel with the modern preoccupation with the epistemologically defined problems of meaning and reference has been masterfully told by Richard Rorty in his book, *Philosophy and the Mirror of Nature*.[1] Our project in the present context is not that of rehearsing the story that Rorty has told so well, but it is rather that of ferreting out the presuppositions of the theoretico-epistemological paradigm that are principally responsible for its resultant aporias in addressing the issues of meaning and reference. This will set the agenda for a discovery of a more suitable matrix for addressing the issues. Our central argument will be that this more suitable matrix is found within the space of communicative praxis.[2]

The fate of meaning and reference within the disciplinary matrix of modern epistemology has been that of a gravitation into a maelstrom of paradoxes and aporias. This has been the case in the traditions of both continental rationalism and British empiricism. Rationalism gravitated into a performative contradiction of looking for that which it had already presumptively found; empiricism landed in the predicament of not being able to find that which it was presumptively looking for. But the bugbear at issue was common to both approaches. It had to do with the shared presupposition that meaning and reference, either already found or yet to be found, were hard-knob determinables. Criteriologically defined in advance, they were deemed to be in possession of the traits of objectifiability, self-identity, and universalizability.

This presupposition as to the nature and status of meaning and reference played itself out in the empiricist tradition in such a manner as to produce undecidability as regards matters of meaning and inscrutability as regards matters of reference. Proceeding from the bare particularity of sense impressions ("sense-qualia" in the grammar of positivism), devoid of all intentionality, empiricism was unable to nail down the proper objects of its investigations. There was nothing universalizable down the road. All that lay ahead were collections of abstracted sensory particulars, ever changing, as they "pass, repass, glide away, and mingle in an infinite variety of postures and situations"—as Hume so eloquently stated the matter in *A Treatise of Human Nature*.[3]

The abstract empiricism of isolated and atomistic sense impressions was tethered to a species of psychologism in the guise of a foundational science. Logic was viewed as a branch of psychology. Logical truths of evidence, inference, and generalization were seen as grounded in psychological acts. John Stuart Mill pushed psychologism to its limits in his *System of Logic* by construing the law of noncontradiction as one of our earliest generalizations from experience. In thus reducing all laws of logic to psychological laws, necessity to contingency, and apodictic certainty to the *feeling* of certainty, the empiricist was unable to find a place for meaning and reference that bore the marks of the sought-after constancy, universalizability, and necessity. Measured against theses strict criteria, meaning was destined to remain undecidable and reference inscrutable.

The rationalist tradition was dedicated to the task of refuting the empiricists' epistemology of sensory-based experience and psychological foundations. Edmund Husserl's contribution in this regard was of particularly unique moment. His celebrated attack on psychologism in his classical work *Logical Investigations* demonstrated quite decisively that the logical and epistemic criteria for meaning and reference could never be met through an empirical observation of psychological acts. Psychology deals with natural laws that are contingent; logic deals with normative laws that are necessary. Logic has a distinct task in investigating the truth content of intellectual acts, the act-intentionality of the cogito. Its task needs to be distinguished from an empirical investigation of the causal origin of intellectual acts. Apodictic evidence is apriori rather than aposteriori. The certainty of proof and justification antedates the *feeling* of certainty.

It is along these lines that Husserl's attack on psychologism unfolds, proceeding from the protocols of a logic-based theory of judgment instead of from an empirical observation of psychological acts. But that which needs to be noted at this juncture is that the basic presupposition of the contending parties, the rationalists on the one hand and the empiricists on the other hand, remains intact. The meaning of meaning carries with it claims for universality and necessity, if not of a metaphysical clearly of an epistemological sort. The question then remains whether such a criteria of meaning can indeed be achieved in our philosophical discourse. We have already noted that the empiricist has chosen to remain skeptical on this matter. Yet to be examined is where the ruminations of a rationalist epistemology lead us.

Might it be that the rationalist epistemology leads us to the same environs as did the empiricist epistemology, namely to the dead ends of an undecidability with respect to meaning and an inscrutability with respect to reference. In its efforts to capture meaning and harness reference through appeals to doctrines of essence, apriori and universal conditions, and invariant rules of inference, rationalism succumbed to the aporias of representationalism and the illusions of foundationalism. Theories of meaning based on a doctrine of essence make purchases on the universalizability of meaning through a procedure of *representation*. A doctrine of essence travels hand in glove with a claim that a meaning that was present in a given context can be *re-presented* in another context. But that which remains problematic in such a putative state of affairs is not only the possibility of retrieving or repeating a presentation that is no longer present in its presentational immediacy, but indeed the sense of what it means to experience "presence" in its alleged original presentment. On this particular point, Jacques Derrida's broadside attack on representational theories of essence and meaning merits particular attention.[4] Although Derrida's specific target is Husserl's construal of meaning and representation, implications abound for any claims for a representational theory of knowledge, be they rationalistic or empiricistic. And again we see how the vagaries of modern rationalism and empiricism, although differing in some significant details end up pretty much in the same ball park as regards presuppositions for a project of epistemological grounding. The bugbear for both is the elusive nature of a foundational *presence*—and here it matters not whether the sought-after presence be that of a universally reclaimable essence, an apriori rule, or a discrete and granular sensory impression.

What may, however, still hang in the balance is whether or not Husserl's later phenomenological project remains immune to the criticisms that Derrida offers in response to Husserl's earlier project. Husserl may indeed remain an "epistemologist" until the bitter end, but if so he becomes quite chastened and restrained in his later work, *The Crisis of European Sciences and Transcendental Phenomenology*. It is here that he informs the reader that his earlier project of "Philosophy as a Rigorous Science" is a dream that has been dreamed out. The earlier project that responded to the call of *"Zu den Sachen selbst"* becomes tempered with a *"Rückgang auf die Lebenswelt."* This "return to the lifeworld," in the aftermath of its objectivization and occlusion of the functioning intentionality of concrete lifeworld experiences, does appear to make all things new with regard to any philosophical project of the future. It is not that "rationality" is now somehow left behind, but rather that the naive rationalism of modern epistemology is placed into question.[5]

It is thus that deliberations on the status of meaning and reference in the epistemological paradigm of modernity appear to stand at an impasse. Neither modern rationalism nor modern empiricism seem to have the resources to secure reliable criteria of meaning and trustworthy strategies of reference. The search for epistemic foundations, either of an empirical or transcendental sort, has resulted in failure. The indeterminacy of cognitive processes appears to have won the day. The very science of epistemology as the *logos* of *epistēmē,* as a reconstruction of the foundations of the act of knowing, has gravitated into philosophical incoherence. To inquire about knowing *that* one knows and *what* it is that one knows when one knows, involves one in a circularity of reasoning which, at best, perpetually defers that which is sought after and, at worst, involves one in a quite blatant performative contradiction. The modern theoretico-epistemological paradigm seems indeed to have become profoundly problematized.

Against the backdrop of these internal developments within the modernity problematic itself, which have brought all efforts at achieving meaning and reference under suspicion, our response is not that of a quick and facile jettisoning of the issues at stake in the pursuit of meaning and reference (as some of our more vocal postmodernist friends have recommended), but rather that of recontextualizing and refiguring the issues involved in the problem as traditionally defined. The theoretic-epistemological paradigm of modernity may indeed have depleted its own resources because of a too heavy investment in theory. But from this we need not draw the conclusion that the usages "to mean" and "to refer" ought to be excised from the philosophical lexicon. We will still continue to make use of the vocabulary of meaning and reference, and we have no animosity against talk about "knowing" this and that. The rejection of epistemology as a foundational science does not entail an elimination of knowledge. We will continue to know much about many things in quite ordinary senses of knowing.

The displacement of meaning and reference as protocols of pure theory, devised in the interests of epistemological grounding, does not in our view entail a rejection of meaning and reference in every sense possible. Admittedly, meaning and reference as a display of bold metaphysical and epistemological exercises may well have outworn its usefulness, but there is another role that these concepts, which are deeply ingrained in our everyday discourse and action, can perform. This role is of a more socio-pragmatic sort in which meaning and reference are seen as traces that provide apertures for a discernment and evaluation of the discourse and action that comprise our quotidian existence. Our central thesis, which we are now able to formulate as an alternative to the theory-laden approach of modern epistemology, is that the issues pertaining to meaning and reference can be creatively rethought by refiguring them within the space of communicative praxis. We are motivated by the call for a *return to praxis*—which may find a certain analog in Husserl's celebrated *"return to the lifeworld"* of his later philosophy. The task that we envision is that of tracking the traces of meaning and reference so as to discern their imprints within the concrete lifeworld of our inter-textured discourse and action.

We speak of "traces of" meaning and reference rather than of "criteria for" meaning and reference. The grammar of criteria buys into a morphology of static structures and pregiven conditions that occlude the dynamic functioning of the trace in its spatial and temporal inscriptions. Criteria are theory based and front loaded. They are installed prior to the adventure of meaning disclosure. Traces are affiliates of praxis, resident within the space of the discourses and actions of the concrete lifeworld, always contextualized within the configurations of sense that inform our intertextured speaking and acting. They comport a presignitive and prepredicative intentionality that antedates any objectivating theoretical act-intentionality.

It is of primal importance to recognize the grammar of trace as testifying of an entwinement of temporality and spatiality within the texture that binds meaning and reference. And this brings us to one of the pivotal and highly suggestive notions invented by Mikhail M. Bakhtin, namely *"the chronotope."* The chronotope, as the peculiar time-space field of the "dialogic imagination" is an assimilation of historical time and historical space. Quite clearly, time and space, within Bakhtin's scheme of things, is not time and space under the guise of a *mathesis universalis*—objectively measured and dissected into discrete instants and points. We are not here dealing with the time of clocks and calendars and the space of geometrical lengths and distances. We are dealing instead with historically lived time and space—time and space as existential coordinates that configure our social practices. Time and space in Bakhtin's economy of the chronotope are from bottom up *lived* time and *lived* space.[6]

It is in this dynamic chronotope that meaning and reference live and move and have their being. The project of tracking meaning and reference is thus that of discerning their traces within a heteroglossia of voices that bespeak patterns of perception, configurations of values, and aesthetic sentiments—and all this against the backdrop of historical memories and anticipations. In such a chronotopal economy meaning and reference are understood as socially and historically imbued practices rather than as achievements of a solitary mental act. They stand in the service of praxis rather than theory. At issue here is not a subject-centered mental operation in the form of a Cartesian ego-cogito, a Kantian transcendental subject, or a Humean sensing self as a bundle of perceptions. Meaning and reference become operative within a wider context of communicative associations. One can well speak of this wider context as a *praxial chronotope.*

THE TURN TO LANGUAGE

The turn to language in the interests of solving the entwined epistemological problematic of meaning and reference ought be neither puzzling nor unexpected. A claim for the inseparability of language from meaning and reference strikes one as approximating a truism. It is in and through language that we articulate meaning and it is in and through language that we designate objects of reference. So much would appear to be quite self-evident. That language should play a role in the quest for meaning and reference would surely seem to be uncontroversial. However, matters become somewhat murky when the issue is raised as to how language might play its invited role. How is language at issue in the achievement of meaning and in the postulates of reference?

Traveling a bit further with Bakhtin's vocabulary of the chronotope we find a veritable heteroglossia of voices seeking to instruct us on the way to language. There are the voices of linguistic science, the voices of structuralist philosophy of language, the voices of Oxford ordinary language analysis, and the voices of a Heideggerian call to language as the "house of Being." In the kingdom of language there indeed appear to be many, many mansions!

We need to begin with some distinctions. There is language as spoken, language as written, language as a system of semiotic units (phonemes, morphemes, and lexemes), language as a rostrum of syntactical rules, and language in the bounds of narrativity. The Saussurian distinction between *parole* and *langue* provides a convenient starting point, although it may not do as an end point. There are the events of speaking and writing a spoken tongue, and there is language as a linguistic structure. And then there is *discourse*—which we submit is the *concrete amalgam of the events of speaking and the structure of language within a social practice.* Neither isolated empirical speech acts nor the abstracted components of semiotic units and syntactical rules in themselves make up the fabric of discourse. Herein resides the limitation of speech-act theory on the one hand and structural linguistics on the other hand. Discourse antedates the abstractive maneuvers of empiricism and linguistic science alike.

The performance of discourse plays itself out as an articulation, a showing, a making manifest of variegated forms of life and styles of existence. Discourse comports a sense of *what* is being said and deploys a saying of something *about* something. It unfolds as an august event in which a semantics of utterance and a strategy of reference are amalgamated. Thus we see that already in this linguistic moment, fleshed out broadly as a moment of discursive praxis, the traces of meaning and reference become discernible.

This performativity of linguistic meaning and reference in our quotidian discursive practices, however, moves about within a broader space of textuality and narrativity. The sentential level of discourse is taken up into an embodiment of texts and an emplotment of stories already told and yet to be told. Ultimately we need to attend to the traces of linguistic meaning and reference in the various forms of emplotment that engage us as narrating beings. As *homo narrans* we are destined to tell the stories of our lives as we at once discover and constitute our world.

The contribution of the French philosopher Paul Ricoeur to an elucidation of the dynamics of narrativity as a strategy of emplotment has been considerable and noteworthy. Seeking to attenuate the conflict of existential-phenomenological with scientific-cosmological time, Ricoeur works out from a reconfigured Aristotelian definition of plot which he then grafts on to an Augustinian notion of time to provide a schema of signification that plays itself out both in fictive and historical narration.[7] The point that needs to be emphasized at this juncture is that the semantics of linguistic meaning and reference plays in a broader arena. It requires a more expansive horizon than the space of phonemes, lexemes, and even sentences. The horizon in which the traces of meaning and reference are discernible includes the region of texts and narratives. Words and sentences are taken up into texts, and texts are taken up into narratives.

In this process of linguistic *Aufhebung,* meaning and reference are themselves refigured. Meaning partakes of a holistic configuration of sense, and reference reaches toward a world in which a heteroglossia of voices and a heterogeneity of stories are inscribed. Texts and narratives are clearly *about* something, but this aboutness is never exhausted by a sentential reference that can provide only cinematographic profiles of particularized speech acts.

This appeal to a broader horizon of language as text and narrative is indicative of certain limitations in the semiotic model in coming to terms with the problem of meaning and reference. These limitations are tied to the methodological decision that semiotics makes in opting for an elementaristic analysis of the constitutive signs used in discourse. Within such a model lexemes become peculiar "word atoms," and phonemes and morphemes are called upon to provide an accompanying "subatomic" infrastructure. Linguistic science, guided by the semiotic model, proceeds via a dissection, atomization, and binary opposition of the constitutive elements that make up language as a system of signs. Within such a methodological matrix, questions regarding the voice of the speaker and the object of reference are necessarily bracketed. The investigations are restricted to the relations among the elemental signs themselves, yielding the special sciences of phonemics, morphology, lexicography, syntactics, and general grammar.

Plainly enough, these special sciences retain their own legitimacy and methodological integrity. The objectification of language as a relational complex of signs, decontextualized and set at a distance from the performances of speaking subjects and the intentionality of reference, is not only permissible but is indeed a requirement for the doing of linguistics as a science. The point at issue here is not that linguistic science lacks an internal justification but rather that the *event-character* of discourse within the holistic configurations of narrative recontextualizes and refigures the sign system of semiotics into a dynamic interplay of traces of meaning and reference. It is only when one moves from phonemes to words and then to sentences and texts, and finally to narratives, that meaning and reference as praxial accomplishments can become an issue. It is important, however, that we not construe this "movement" from semiotic units to narratives as a linear and progressive development that proceeds from an infrastructural base to a superstructural derivative. What is operative here is a transversal envelopment rather than a successive development.

It is only within this dynamic interplay of the events of discourse and narration that the workings of meaning and reference are robustly illustrated, and they are illustrated in such a guise as to engender a vortex of intentionalities that push beyond the language-bound space of discourse, textuality, and narrative itself. This brings us to a crucial juncture in our interpretive analysis—the juncture at which the economy of meaning and reference opens out to a region on the hither side of language itself. Language may indeed go all the way down and all the way back in our quest for meaning, but one needs to stop short of any claims that meaning and reference are nothing more than the offspring of language endeavors and that there is nothing *outside of* or *exterior to* language. The Bakhtinian chronotope with its assimilated historical time and space provides for a disclosure of a wider region of forces at work in our making of sense and our referring. It is within this chronotope that the concrete lifeworld of our amalgamated discourse and action becomes visible, opening a wider region for our explorations of the traces of meaning and reference.

It should be mentioned at this juncture that in the travails of the linguistic turn the Ordinary Language School (sometimes identified as the School of Oxford Analysis) has been more promising than the semiotic approach of structuralist linguistics in beckoning us back to the concrete lifeworld. And in assisting us in this regard its proponents have been helpful in pointing out certain misdirections by the epistemologists of sense and reference from Frege to Russell and beyond. Ordinary language, in the locution of the alleged founder of the Ordinary Language School, Ludwig Wittgenstein, is a "form of life" *(Lebensform).* Its meanings and references are ensconced in our everyday usages as we seek to make our way about in the discourses and actions within our civil society.

Returning to language as a form and feature of the concrete life-world, we come to more fully understand the failures on the part of both modern epistemologists and structural linguists to recognize that sense and reference are dependent upon a rhetorically discursive context of addressor/addresee interaction. The identification of sense and the determination of reference remain contextualized within the contingencies of rhetorical engagements. Meaning and reference cannot be established for all times and all places. They are situationally conditioned, emergents from speaker/interlocutor exchanges and responses to the particular state of affairs at issue. And it is this contextuality and contingency traveling with our signifiers and signifieds that alerts us to the sirens of impermeable consensus on the one hand and anarchic dissensus on the other hand, both as artificial linguistic-epistemological constructs.

Stanley Cavell has been particularly helpful on this issue in his Wittgensteinian effort to rescue "criteria" in our making sense and in our referring from the clutches of the epistemological-criteriological construct of modern theory of knowledge. Criteria are seen no longer as standards for apodictic certainty, grounding incontrovertible evidence and unimpeachable truth-conditions, but are viewed rather as rhetorical strategies in language as a form of life for showing that something "consists in" or "counts as" something. We will then be able to discern, writes Cavell, that what is at issue in epistemological theory-construction of criteria is "just the ordinary rhetorical structure of the ordinary word 'criteria'."[8]

THE DEMAND FOR A HERMENEUTICAL PHENOMENOLOGY

The coupling of language and the lifeworld, occasioned by our turn/return to Bakhtin's suggestive notion of the chronotope as an intersection of lived historical time with lived historical space, and encouraged by Wittgensteinian ruminations on language as a form of life, leads us to an acknowledgment of the demand for a hermeneutical phenomenology. Now to call upon the resources of an approach that is at once hermeneutical and phenomenological in addressing the meaning/reference problematic would appear to catapult one into a situation of semantic dissonance resulting from a clash of vocabularies. Do not hermeneutics and phenomenology provide us with diverse philosophical perspectives that resist any collaboration in a common philosophical quest? Is not the method of phenomenological description and constitution, which is very much a strategy of subject-centered epistemological inquiry, at odds with the hermeneutical task of antifoundationalist understanding and interpretation? How can epistemologically based description and constitution collaborate with hermeneutically oriented understanding and interpretation in a common philosophical endeavor?

Our position is one that sees the phenomenological and hermeneutical as entwined polar moments that reinforce each other, providing new perspectives on what we mean in our discourse and our action and how we refer to the contents of what we say and do. The phenomenological moment provides the occasion for the recontextualiztion and refiguration of meaning and reference against the backdrop of the notion of intentionality and the phenomenon of the lifeworld. The hermeneutical moment supplies the strategies for understanding and interpretation that are always already at work in the intentionality that stimulates any phenomenological description and analysis of traces of meaning and reference.

Our use of the notion of intentionality clearly draws its inspiration from the seminal phenomenological reflections of Edmund Husserl, as does also our appeal to the grammar of a lifeworld *(Lebenswelt)*. However, in our own phenomenological reconstruction these two pivotal notions do not come to rest with the peculiar results of Husserl's explorations. We move out from Husserl's notion of intentionality, and indeed that of Franz Brentano from an earlier time, but we do not stay with their epistemological construal of its workings. We appropriate the fundamental feature of intentionality as a "reaching out . . . ," "directed towards . . . ," "appetition for . . . ," but we resituate the fundamental feature within the interstices of a praxis rather than attempting to locate it in a cognitive or mental act. Our notion of intentionality falls out as an explicit *praxial intentionality*. It is not simply nor primordially a cognitive act-intentionality. Admittedly, Husserl already pointed us in the direction of a more praxis-oriented notion of intentionality with his concept of "functioning intentionality" *(fungierende Intentionalität)*, but he was never wholly successful in liberating this functioning intentionality from its Cartesian and Kantian epistemological attachments. It remained at best a supplement to theoretico-epistemological act-intentionality.

Intentionality as a deployment of meaning is inseparable from social practices. It gathers into its inscriptions the legacy of a tradition and a cultural milieu from which all discourse and action proceed. The meaning of a portion of discourse or a plan of action resides as much in the social practices as in the speaking or agentive subject. Intentionality has to do with a configuration of sense that gathers an amalgamated figuration of discourse and action that issues from a situated subject and the sedimented contents of a social and institutional memory. The figure-background entwinement, made so much of in Merleau-Ponty's existential phenomenology of perception, needs to be given its proper due.[9] As the background of the outer horizon in visual perception always already informs the sense of the perceived figure, so the background of cultural forms and historical memories at every step informs the inscription of meaning in our life of praxial engagements. It is this meeting of figure and background that occasions the achievement of meaning as an event of configuration.

This event of configuration, it is important to emphasize, never remains closed in upon itself. It is always a reaching out, an opening toward, a breaking through beyond its own limits of inscription. It is at once a *preservation* and *repetition* of discourse and action, through which such discourse and action is perpetually reclaimed, and a *refiguration* and *transformation* of this discourse and action through the projection of new possibilities. Intentionality repeats and refigures the *Sache* of discourse, its sense and reference, within the life of thought and action.

The second decisive feature of phenomenological philosophy, traveling with praxial intentionality, is the notion of the lifeworld. This notion too was inspired by Husserl, and particularly by his later phenomenological reflections and his proposal for a *Rückgang auf die Lebenswelt*. But here also, as in our critical appropriation of Husserl's concept of intentionality, we wish to offer an amendment that effectively deprogrammatizes Husserl's transcendental phenomenology. The amendment comes in the form of a deconstruction of the transcendental-phenomenological paradigm of knowledge in which the lifeworld appears as the last noema in the odyssey of a transcendental reduction that moves from objectivity to subjectivity to intersubjectivity and eventually to the data of the lifeworld. We propose a refiguration of the lifeworld as proper referent.

Praxial intentionality achieves fulfillment not in picking out the lifeworld as noematic object or intended essence, but rather in the lifeworld as a field of praxis in which the inscriptions of discourse and action are always already ensconced. No longer proffered as the end result of a *Letztbegrundung,* the lifeworld now emerges as the ever-expanding horizon of our everyday practices as they are con-textualized against the background of an historical tradition and a foreground of historical anticipations. The lifeworld functions no longer as an epistemological or metaphysical principle of grounding but is seen rather as an attestation of a socio-historical world of dis-cursive and nondiscursive practices. In short, the lifworld descends into history.

The peculiar relevance of the phenomenological notions of inten-tionality and the lifeworld for our current project is that they can aid us in sketching the traces of meaning and reference by citing the con-tributions of the speaking and acting subject and by pointing to an opening that leads beyond the "world of the text" to the wider world of lived experience. To be sure, praxial intentionality is always con-textual-ized, unfolding within configurations of text and narrative; but it is not reducible to text and narrative. It furrows paths to the life of a speaking and acting subject and a lifeworld as the referent of that which is spoken about. This lifeworld was at most only adum-brated in our considerations of the epistemological and linguistic traces of meaning and reference.

In moving to the hermeneutical moment in our genealogy of meaning and reference, another set of considerations come into play. It is here that the role of interpretation becomes explicit, and the major lesson to be learned at this juncture is that interpretation goes all the way down and all the way back. This becomes evident as we monitor the slide of hermeneutics into linguistics, semiotics, textual-ity, and narrativity. The alleged "facts" within a semiotic system of phonemes and lexemes do not fall from heaven as pure data. They become facts only within a disciplinary matrix constituted by a com-munity of investigators intent on institutionalizing the various sub-disciplines of linguistic science—phonemics, morphology, lexicography, and syntactics. And such a community of investigators is at once a community of interpreters. The constitution of a disciplinary matrix is at the same time a project of interpretation.

For example, interpretation is already in play in the flagging of certain lexical entries as being of current usage, archaic, or indeed obsolete. Interpretation is in play in the decision to include certain items in the lexicon and exclude others. Interpretation is in play in the decision to terminate the list of entries and consider the lexicon finished. Interpretation is in play in the accommodating of grammar to current usage. In all this, interpretation is operative. The definition and location of signs within the endless semiotic play of signifiers and signifieds is the progeny of interpretation. Signs are themselves constituted in and through the workings of the "hermeneutical as" (which is itself always already operative in the "apophantic as"). Signs are *taken as* elements and functions that have a measure of explanatory power within a semiotic system that comprises language as an object.

Interpretation is at work not only on the semiotic level but also in the "world" of the text and within the economy of narratives. The texts that we compose and the stories that we tell unfold as profiles of interpretive understanding. Here, too, the "hermenetuical as" is operative. The messages of texts and narratives are the result of a Gadamerian "fusion of horizons" through which multiple interpretive perspectives fuse and diffuse, intermingle and separate, mutually correcting each other. Language, texts, and narratives are never mere objects, simple juxtapositions of elemental units. Nor are they mere media, transmitters of information, containers of ideas, or external garments that clothe our thoughts. Infused with interpretation, they are more properly viewed as events within a field of communicative praxis, comporting a praxial intentionality that discloses a lifeworld of practical concerns.

When the language/text/narrative configuration is properly seen as a holistic event rather than as a serialization of regimens of discrete data, the splintering off of language, textuality, and narrative from the related disciplines of history, sociology, anthropology, psychology, and political science is effectively curtailed. This places upon hermeneutics an explicit multidisciplinary demand. The scene of interpretation is indeed a global one, in which the phenomenological concept of the lifeworld is refigured as a socio-historical world and the project of hermeneutics is redefined along the lines of an explicit *cultural* hermeneutics. This refiguration of world and hermeneutics alike broadens the space of the genealogy of meaning and reference, making possible an elucidation of their workings within an expanded historical consciousness.

This brings us to the decisive feature of the hermeneutical moment—the placement of interpretation squarely within the workings of an historical consciousness within a socio-historical world. The implications of this for our account of meaning and reference are at once direct and obvious. The traces of meaning and reference that we have followed over the terrains of epistemology, linguistics, semiotics, narrativity, and phenomenology now point us in the direction of an historically imbued consciousness within an historically imbued world. It is here that meaning and reference refigure themselves again—as at once event of recollection and anticipation, retention and protention, commemoration and hope. The socio-historical world of lived-through practices, implicating a decentered and engaged consciousness, is textured against the background of a traditon extending into the past and a foreground of expectations projecting into a future. The historical chronotope of the socio-historical world provides the points and lines of intersection of facticity and novelty, givenness and openness, preservation and invention.

It is within this Bakhtinian chronotopal expanse, binding past and future, that meaning and reference are operative. The "what" around which our discourse turns and the "that" to which it refers display the ingression of a past and a repetition of that which has been. To this extent Hegel was right: *Wesen ist was gewesen ist*. The performances of meaning and reference are recollective operations. However, these recollective operations are not to be construed as retrievals of eternal and untrammeled essences, situated on the hither side of temporal becoming. They are operations that effect a repetition of configurations of social practices that have already become inscribed into the texture of the socio-historical world. Recollection issues from *dieseits* rather than *jenseits* the travail of historical becoming.

What is of particular significance at this juncture is that the classical doctrine of recollection is at once demetaphysicalized and deepistemologized as a strategy of theoretical recognition and placed squarely within the space of praxial intentionality.[10] This flags the transition of hermeneutics "beyond epistemology," interpretation no longer being defined as a mental act (or a set of mental acts) but rather as an assemblage of social practices. In this move hermeneutics takes on a new face and a new posture, jettisoning its alignment with modern epistemological theory of mind (as was still the case with the tradition of idealist hermeneutics from Schleiermacher through Dilthey) and becoming repostured as *cultural* hermeneutics.

The recollection of historical consciousness, however, is but one side of the proverbial two-sided coin. The performance of recollection is always intertwined with anticipatory projection. Historical consciousness is at once recollective and anticipatory. The traces of meaning and reference in this historical consciousness point to a future as well as to a past, setting the requirement for a continuing redescription of those meanings and referents that have already become sedimented in the socio-historical world. Meaning and reference thus take on the character of an open texture, ever subject to expansion, revision, or indeed overturn. No meanings and references are ever finalized, fixed, and finished. This introduces a factor of indeterminacy in all of our claims for meaning and reference. Our strategies for determinate renderings are always delimited by the not yet said and the not yet done. But there is also a more positive feature of the open texture of our historical consciousness. Not only does it delimit the weight of the tradition and recollection, it also sets possibilities for a reappropriation of the effects of the past and a reinscription of their significance in light of the requirements for future oriented thought and action. Historical consciousness has a future so as not to succumb to the destiny of the past.

We can now summarize the results of our peculiar genealogy of meaning and reference. Our central task has been to dislodge the issues of meaning and reference from the theoretico-epistemological paradigm that has determined the development of these issues since the advent of modern philosophy, and to resituate them within the hermeneutical space of praxial intentionality. Meaning and reference have been removed from their epistemological space and reinserted into a hermeneutical space. This shift may indeed involve, as Paul Ricoeur has maintained in his monumental three-volume work *Time and Narrative,* a substitution of the grammar of a configuration/refiguration interplay for the epistemological protocols of modernity. Ricoeur finds the interplay of configuration and refiguration most effectively illustrated in the mimetic emplotment of narrativity. His use of the resources of narrativity in transfiguring the meaning/reference problematic is both bold and philosophically imaginative.

Yet, we have some concerns about the tendency in his thought to over-extend the parameters of narrativity As Derrida has informed us that "there is nothing outside the text,"[11] so Ricoeur at times comes perilously close to the view that there is nothing outside the narrative. This is a pitfall that needs to be avoided. In all fairness to Ricoeur, however, it should be pointed out that at the conclusion of his extensive study on temporality and narrativity he does recognize the need to delimit the use of the internal resources of narrational emplotment in one's effort to deal with the mystery of time. "Not even narrative," he writes at the end of his treatise, "exhausts the power of the speaking that refigures time."[12] An element of inscrutability remains in our dealings with time. Narrativity by itself cannot surmount the aporia of temporality.

Our contention throughout has been that there is indeed a socio-historical world of praxis outside the text and outside the narrative. The integrity of the intentionality of our social practices and the resilient referentiality of the lifeworld resists all efforts toward textual and narratological closure. Our explorations have led us through the thicket of epistemological foundationalism, to language, to phenomenology, and finally to hermeneutics. This journey, it is hoped, has opened up a perspective on the chronotope of our lived socio-historical world with its amalgam of discourse and action. And only on the terrain of this vibrant lifeworld do the traces of meaning and reference lead anywhere.

ESSAY II

The Subject in Question and the Question about the Questioner

HISTORICAL BACKGROUNDS

IF THERE ARE SUCH ENTITIES as historical facts in the discipline of philosophy, I would submit that the recent accelerated questioning of the status and role of the human subject qualifies as one of them. The subject has been placed into question in a quite unprecedented manner. Indeed, in some philosophical circles the very use of the grammars of "subject" and "subjectivity" are bound to elicit raised eyebrows. Such is particularly the case within the enclaves of deconstructionist and postmodernist thought, where the prevailing attitude is that traditional signifiers like "subject," "ego," "self," "mind"—to say nothing of the slippery eel, "human nature"—have outworn their usefulness. The more vocal representatives of the deconstructionist persuasion are convinced that these signifiers were devoid of utility from the very beginning, ever in want of a determination of that which is allegedly signified. So it is laconically proclaimed that the "death of the subject" was prefigured quite before its invention.

Michel Foucault's role in the telling of the story of the invention and demise of the subject has for some time now been referenced across the disciplines, and particularly in the fields of literary theory and the human sciences. Practitioners in these fields repeatedly remind us of Foucault's pronouncement at the conclusion of *The*

19

Order of Things, where he informs his readers that "man" is an "invention of recent date" that is soon "to be erased like a face drawn in the sand at the edge of the sea."[13] Now Foucault is able to write about "man" as a recent invention because what he has in mind is the Kantian philosophical anthropology in which the human self is defined as occupying an interstitial space within the hollow of an empirico-transcendental doublet. But quite before the advent of transcendental philosophy with its attempted amalgamation of the empirical and the transcendental, a plethora of philosophies of the human subject had already appeared on the scene. And one would surely not be all that far amiss in tracing the parentage of the spate of Western philosophical reflection on the nature and destiny of the human subject to the ancient Socratic dictum "Know Thyself!"

Although the concept of the human subject in the history of Western philosophy cannot become the specific focus of our current project, it needs to remain in the background of all reflections on the subject and subjectivity, both past and present. Of specific relevance in any consideration of this background is the bold application of the metaphysical categories of substance and attribute in seeking to come to terms with the Socratic requirement of achieving self-knowledge. Such was particularly the case in ancient and medieval philosophy where the Greek concept of the psyche as a soul-substance provided the answer to the question as to what it means to exist as a human being among the furniture of the totality of beings that populate the cosmos. Every schoolboy of course knows how badly the application of the traditional category of substance in an investigation of the being and behavior of the human self fared in the modern period, thanks principally to the empiricist critique of David Hume and the transcendental critique of Immanuel Kant.

But prior to the well-rehearsed developments of empiricism and rationalism initiated by Hume and Kant, there occurred the invention of the modern concept of mind by the alleged founder of modern philosophy, René Descartes. And surely Descartes's formulation of the problem at issue played a role in the critical responses of Hume and Kant as well as among the legion of naysayers within the contemporary deconstructionist enclave. With his celebrated doctrine of the *ego-cogito,* Descartes sought to secure a stable foundation for the *res cogitans* as a nonextended thing that thinks, which he facilely differentiated from the *res extensa* as the modality of being that defined the bits and pieces of the world that are extended but do not think. Through these maneuvers, as is well known, Descartes became the inventor of modern philosophy of mind, defining the thinking subject as a mental substance.

It was Descartes's doctrine of mind as mental substance that became the intractable bugbear for both Hume and Kant, albeit for different reasons. Hume's doctrine of the self as a bundle of perceptions, as this doctrine was elaborated in his *Treatise of Human Nature,* could find no place for the metaphysical simplicity and personal self-identity of a Cartesian mental substance. According to Hume, what we are left with after the dust of our philosophical reflections has settled is a self in perpetual flux and movement, in which its fleeting perceptions succeed each other with an astonishing rapidity, never coming to rest in a stable state of affairs. Kant, although somewhat more charitable to the classical doctrine of substance allowing it a certain regulative function, is nonetheless equally strident in his attack on any position that claims to have constitutive knowledge of the self as an abiding and self-identical substance, somehow "standing-under" its changing attributes.

THE CONTEMPORARY SCENE

In moving to the contemporary scene of the portrayal of the fortunes and misfortunes of the human subject one quickly finds that this scene becomes intelligible only against the backdrop of classical and modern inquiries, in which the categories of substance and attributes were very much at issue. A distinctive feature of the contemporary scene is the colorful variety of approaches and positions, often aligned with geographical variations. We speak of Continental and Anglo-analytical approaches to the issue, and there are claims for a quite distinctive take on the matter by American pragmatism. And within and across these geographical parameters there are the approaches of the early and the later schools of Analytical Philosophy; the early and later programs of Phenomenology; the approach of Process Philosophy; the explorations of Existentialism; the interrogations of the School of Critical Theory; the way of Hermeneutics; the reactive postures of Deconstruction and Postmodernism—and no doubt garden varieties of each and in some cases possible combinations of all!

To render an account of each of these contemporary perspectives would indeed be a worthy project, but given the constraints of a single lecture our focus will need to be much more narrowly defined. Given that our friends of deconstruction have offered the most strident assaults on the grammar of subjectivity, putting the subject "in question" in a quite radical manner, it might be of some interest to begin with them—without any assurance, however, that we will end with them! Jacques Derrida, commonly acclaimed to be the "father of deconstruction" (although mistakenly so), has been explicit in his mapping of a strategy in which any claims for a philosophy of the subject are undermined. And what one notices, and almost straightway, is that in Derrida's deconstruction of the subject, it is principally a Cartesianlike ego-cogito that falls under indicment; although clearly the classical versions of the subject, appealing to an underlying *hypokeimenon,* do not fare much better. In any event, it soon becomes evident that one will not succeed in making much sense out of the Derridean project if it is decontextualized from the history of Western philosophy. And in noting this we become aware that it was not Derrida but rather Heidegger who needs to be accorded the notoriety of launching the project of deconstruction. *Abbau* was Heidegger's name for this project, making it quite clear, and particularly in *The Basic Problems of Phenomenology,* that the required philosophical task is "a critical process in which the traditional concepts, which at first must necessarily be employed, are de-constructed down to the sources from which they were drawn."[14]

Heidegger's strategy of deconstruction proceeds with the ontological-ontic difference as its principal wrecking tool. What needs to be dismantled, according to Heidegger, is the history of Western metaphysics as an ontic enterprise, a preoccupation with the economy of beings from the lowest to the highest, at the expense of forgetting the question about the Being *(Sein)* that is at issue in every particular being *(Seiendes)* that comes into view. He called this the "forgetfulness of Being" *(Vergessenheit des Seins).* Derrida transposed Heidegger's ontological-ontic difference into a grammatological key and reconfigured the project of deconstruction into one that was driven by the workings of *differance*—at once a "differing from" and a "deferring." The implications of this reconfigured project for the fate of the human subject are quite far reaching.

It will remain the case for any self-respecting Derridean that any effort to lay hold of an abiding and self-identical subject will end in failure for want of trustworthy signifiers and signifieds. Again, it is the Cartesian subject that looms in the background as the principal vagary. In the doctrine of the Cartesian subject we find a rather bold claim for an abiding *presence,* a psychic basement in the guise of a mental substance that underlies the changing attributes of perception, imagination, and conception. To grasp the essence of this self-identical mental substance an act of self-reflection is required, enabling the self to become present to itself in the reflective act. But caught up in the throes of a pervading *differance,* the presence of a self present to itself escapes any and all determinations and remains perpetually deferred. Such is the effect of Derrida's strategy of deconstruction on the life of the human self as subject. Plainly enough, this dismantling of presence entails a deconstruction not only of the Cartesian ego-cogito, but also Kant's transcendental subject, the sensorial subject of Humean empiricism, the Hegelian historical subject as the lynch pin for absolute knowledge—and it would seem pretty much the subject in any sense you please!

Yet, a disclaimer of any total eradication of subject comes from Derrida himself, in his somewhat unexpected reply at the 1966 Johns Hopkins International Symposium on "The Languages of Criticism and the Sciences of Man" to Professor Doubrovsky's concerns about the dissolution of the subject. In a response that initially appears somewhat puzzling, Derrida tells Doubrovsky: "I don't destroy the subject. I situate it. . . . It is a question of knowing where it comes from and how it functions."[15] Now the task of explicating how Derrida "situates" the subject as a "function" against the wider backdrop of his philosophy of *differance* with its deconstruction of presence is a formidable one indeed. Derrida has not gone public on precisely how such a reconciliation of the dissolution of presence with a resituated subject is to proceed. It is thus that one needs to play with some possible interpretations.

Much of the problem has to do with the grammar of "function" itself. One would think that a function would always be a function *of something*—either the function of an underlying substrate or that of a formal structure. The one meaning of function is inscribed in the traditional metaphysical substance/function distinction; the other meaning is exemplified in the structure/function coupling that is very much at the basis of structuralist thought. But surely neither traditional metaphysics nor contemporary structuralism could find a happy home in Derrida's deconstructionist philosophy of *differance.* This would catapult one either into a metaphysics of presence or into a formalism of structure. And it is clearly the case that both of these comprise the principal targets of Derrida's strategic maneuvers.

A possible way out of the dilemma would be to redefine function as grammatological in chararacter and situate the subject as a *function of discourse,* and more specifically as a function of writing *(écriture),* privileging the written text over the spoken word. Given Derrida's repeated harpooning of phonocentrism, such may well be the right interpretive take on the matter. Derrida could quite congenially accept the opening lines of the gospel according to John the Evangelist, "In the beginning was the Word," but he could do so only with the proviso that the "word" that was in the beginning was the written or textualized word rather than the spoken or dialogical word. This enables Derrida to effect a simultaneous deconstruction of logocentrism and phonocentrism. What remains in the aftermath of such a deconstruction is the subject as grammatological function within the space of textuality, recalling what surely is one of the oft-quoted lines from the Derridean corpus: "There is nothing outside the text *(il n'y a pas de hors-texte).*"[16]

Now one may be disposed to agree with Derrida, and the affiliates of deconstruction more generally, that it is not all that productive to continue to appeal to a centered subject in the guise of a Cartesian mental substance, an abiding substratum, or even a stable formal condition ala the transcendental subject of Kant or the web of invariant socio-linguistic relations of structuralism. However, to define the subject solely as a grammatical function, as Derrida is inclined to do, may be too restrictive, leaving us with a subject that is too thin and too vapid to stand as an answer to the multiple profiles of the "who" that quite vigorously poses the question about its status as questioner. The Cartesian subject may indeed have ceased to elicit our interest, but the question about who does the questioning in the wake of the dismantling of the Cartesian ego-cogito is not that easily displaced. Might one be able to take a line from Merleau-Ponty's enunciation that the truth of Husserl's phenomenological reduction resides in the fact that no complete reduction is possible and extend its applicability to the truth of Derrida's deconstruction, explicating its truth value as residing in the fact that no complete deconstruction is possible?

To enable us to productively pursue this line of inquiry it may be helpful to listen to another philosophical voice on the contemporary scene—a voice with which those of you here assembled at Oxford's historic Saint Edmunds Hall are all quite familiar. This is the voice of Gilbert Ryle in his ground-breaking *The Concept of Mind,* published in 1949, in which the principal target is in many respects similar to the one that is singled out by Derrida and his followers. In *The Concept of Mind* it is the Cartesian doctrine of mental substance that comes under brutal attack, and it is the principal project of the work to dispel this myth of the mind as a specter of an intangible substance, a view of mind that has congealed as the peculiar legacy of Descartes's philosophy. The format of Ryle's project unfolds as a contesting of what he names the "official doctrine" on the relation of mind and body, in which mind and body are viewed as distinct and separable entities. In this official doctrine bodies are defined as public entities existing in space, open to inspection by external observers and governed by the laws of mechanics. Mind, in bold contrast to bodies. is defined as a private event, known only through introspection, exempt from all mechanistic explanation—a veritable "ghost in a machine," as Ryle wryly puts it.[17]

Admittedly, having a common target will not make Ryle and Derrida congenial philosophical bedfellows! But there is more in an account of Ryle's philosophical contribution that should be of value to anyone interested in transnational communication. In 1929, twenty years before the publication of his *The Concept of Mind,* Ryle wrote and published one of the very first extensive reviews of Martin Heidegger's *Sein und Zeit.* In this review he provided the reader with a succinct consolidation of the central thrust of Heidegger's celebrated *Abbau.* Heidegger, he writes, is a philosopher who "shows himself to be a thinker of real importance by the immense subtlety and searchingness of his examination of consciousness, by the boldness and originality of his methods and conclusions, and by the *unflagging energy with which he tries to think beyond the stock categories of orthodox philosophy and psychology* (italics mine)."[18]

Plainly enough, Ryle here succeeds in consolidating the strategy of Heidegger's project of deconstruction, articulated as a concerted effort to dismantle the metaphysical categories and epistemological constructs that have informed the history of Western philosophy from its very beginning, and particularly up and through the Cartesian scaffolding of the different kinds of substances. And one surely should not overlook the fact that Ryle himself employed a similar strategy twenty years later in dismantling the Cartesian invention of the mind as a ghost in a machine. To be sure, Ryle's dismantling took an explicit linguistic turn, intent on pointing out how the official doctrine of Cartesian dualism rests on a "category-mistake." Derrida, too, as we have seen, appealed to language for reconfiguring Heidegger's ontological-ontic difference. This is not to say that Ryle's and Derrida's projects are woven from the same cloth. Indeed, there are consequential differences. But what surely should be of some interest is that, on the contemporary philosophical scene, voices from the Continent and the British Isles have converged in pursuing the question about the questioner who places the subject into question.

Toward a Portrait of the Questioner

The contemporary scene, on both sides of the English Channel, beckons us to pursue the status of the questioner who puts the subject in question. And it is surely of some consequence that the site for explorations of the posture and portrait of the questioner is a linguistic terrain, understood in its broadest sense to be sure. The grammatological approach of Derrida, in which the questioner as subject becomes a function of *écriture* is not to be identified with the ordinary language approach of Ryle, in which the move is in the direction of a linguistic behaviorism. Yet, plainly enough, in both cases we are dealing with resources and functions of language. Thus one is able to characterize the common direction in contemporary British and Continental investigations of the topic as that of a linguistic turn.

Common to both, we quickly find, are far-reaching reservations about the utility of a centered subject of consciousness, anchored in a self-identical and underlying substance that stands in support of changing attributes. The subject at the bottom of its being is neither a metaphysical entity nor a transcendental condition. Ryle's linguistic turn is maneuvered quite specifically to call our attention to the category mistake that infects Descartes's doctrine of the subject as a mental substance. Now the category of "mind" apparently still has some utility in Ryle's scheme of things, but we are made to understand that mind/self/subject are not to be construed as a ghost in a machine. The dismantling of this invented apparition, we have suggested, is the key element in Ryle's version of deconstruction.

This facet of his deconstructive strategy is one that we can readily endorse. We have worries, however, about Ryle's reluctance to extend his deconstructive maneuver across the constitutive elements of the Cartesian dualism. If the Cartesian concept of mind as a nonextended thinking substance requires deconstruction, might it not also be the case that the Cartesian invention of the human body as a nonthinking extended substance needs to be deconstructed? Descartes wants to be very clear about the body being an intricate machine subject to the laws of mechanics. This is the other protocol that informs his dualism. On the one hand the mind is understood as an invisible ethereal substance and on the other hand the body is understood as a visible arrangement of interlocking body parts. Might it be that there are two inventions at issue here that need to be called into question, the invention of mind as a ghost in a machine and the invention of the body as a machine in which the ghost resides?

The physiological mechanics that travels with the Cartesian dualism becomes poignantly problematized when one turns one's attention to the body in its enactment of lived-through experiences of touching and being touched, the handshake, the caress, the shaking of the fist in anger and writhing of the body in pain. At issue here is the *body-as-lived* rather than the body as an inert extended substance or a soft machine. As Ryle called our attention to the category mistake in the identification of mind as a mental substance, so we would be well served in recognizing the category mistake of viewing the body-as-lived as an instance of physical bodies in general, defined by the abstracted physical properties of extension and figure, mass and motion. Here too we are bamboozled by taking the representation of a particular event or state of affairs as belonging to one logical type when in fact it belongs to another.

The importance of language, and particularly language in its ordinary and everyday expressiveness, quickly comes to the fore. The requirement is to find an appropriate vocabulary for articulating the embodiment of lived experience in such a wise as to avoid the baneful dualisms of mind and body that reach far back in the tradition of Western thought. Aristotle spoke of the soul being in the body like a pilot being in his ship. Descartes appropriated the metaphor and construed the "being in" of the soul in the body as that of an inherence of a mental substance in a material substance. But what sort of "being in" or "inherence" is at work here? There are multiple senses of "in" that receive expression in our ordinary linguistic usage, and it is difficult to land upon a sense that would fit the entwinement of "lived" and "body" in our concrete embodiment as a *lived body*. As the preposition "in" with its multiple metaphorical extensions appears to occlude the phenomenon at issue, so also is this the case with the metaphors of ownership and possession often invoked in talk about the mind/body relationship. To be sure, one often speaks of "*my* body" and "*having* a body," but one needs be wary of a slide of this ordinary usage into quasi-metaphysical claims that the body is something that one owns, a possession which as the result of certain circumstances happens to belong to one and which could be disposed without serious consequences to the soul's interior being. It is thus that thought experiments with locutions like "I *am* my body" or "I *exist* as embodied' can be helpful in avoiding the lure of sundry metaphysical sirens. The contributions of Gabriel Marcel and Maurice Merleau-Ponty in particular are well known for advancing an elucidation of the multifaceted phenomenon of embodied being-in-the-world.[19]

Our continuation of the conversation with Ryle on matters concerning the status of the questioner thus leads to the concept of embodiment. In Rylean vocabulary one might speak of the phenomenon at issue as "embodied mind," which fills the space vacated as a result of the deconstruction of mind as "ghost in a machine." However, as we have suggested, there is a demand for a second-stage deconstruction whereby the body prejudged as a mechanical arrangement of external parts is dismantled in the interest of making visible the body in its lived concreteness as a holistic site on which projects are to be enacted and tasks are to be performed. The human body needs to be rescued from the snares of a reductive behaviorism—a rescue effort that Ryle was unable to achieve because of a proclivity on his part to move in the direction of a "linguistic behaviorism." The lived body is that place from which human action proceeds—a place that is *inhabited* rather than *occupied* in the manner in which inert objects take up room within abstracted geometrical coordinates. This notion of embodiment in turn provides a sheet anchor against tendencies toward a reductive behaviorism that continues to make purchases on a concept of the human body as a soft machine.

As our critical conversation with Ryle, moving out from the resources of ordinary language analysis on the topic at issue, points us in the direction of a portrait of the questioner as embodied mind, so our visitation of the contributions of Derrida opens an inquiry into the status of the questioner as discursive agent in the performative role of saying something about something. As in our using of Ryle against himself we are seeking to avoid the Sylla of behaviorism, so in using Derrida against himself we are attempting to install safeguards against the Charybdis of pantextualism.

The questioner is embodied mind. This is our first observation in tracking the status of the subject that has placed its own being into question. The questioner is an *embodied* subject. However, the questioner is also, and at the same time as it were, a *discursive* subject, a subject that speaks and writes and in its speaking and writing constitutes itself as subject. The subject is implicated in its discourse, which as discourse is *about* something, *for* someone, and *by* someone. In a previous work we have come to call the implication of the speaking subject an event of "hermeneutical self-implicature." We accentuate the importance of this event so as to avoid the evaporation of the status of speakers and authors in an impenetrable fog of pantextualism. And this provides us with an occasion to be reminded of the insight by the Lebanese linguist Émile Benveniste: "It is in and through language that man constitutes himself as a *subject*. . . . Ego is he who says "ego.""[20] The subject is called into being through language, and more specifically through language as discourse understood as a "saying" or a narrating in which the subject appears on the horizon as a *homo narrans*. This saying, we wish to underscore, is always a saying of something, by someone, for someone. It is thus that the subject will need to be located/relocated within the interstitial spaces overlapping speakers and hearers, authors and readers, rhetors and audiences, citizens and the polis.

This constitution of the subject in and through discourse, it needs to be emphasized, is not the constitution of an interiorized, self-identical, sovereign subject. It is rather a constitution the dynamics of which resides in the potentiality to respond to prior discourse. The who that is speaking defines herself in her response to discourse that is already on the scene—responding to questions that are being asked, commands that are being given, assertions that are being made, moral prescriptions that are being proposed, and aesthetic sentiments that are being expressed. The self-constitution of the subject within the economy of discourse is always a constitution *with* the other. It is this that supplies the weight of alterity in the discursive situation. The questioner, bent on questioning his or her subjectivity, is a discursive questioner incorporated within the discourses of other questioners.

Yet, the discursive questioner as speaking subject is able to mark out its own history, and it does this principally by establishing a critical distance in the dialogic encounter. There is admittedly a consummate reciprocity operative within the concrete density of the dialogical interaction of self with other self, making difficult any clear-cut distinction between what is "mine" and what is "yours." In dialoging with you I lend you my thoughts as I receive yours; and you lend me your thoughts as you receive mine, as we move back and forth, sometimes agreeing, other times dissenting, and still other times modifying what each of us has contributed so as to effect a new slant or perspective on the issues at hand.

The dynamics of dialogue is such that the thoughts and articulations of speaker and interlocutor feed upon each other, and it is only after we do a postmortem on the dialogue that we are able to sort out the episodical histories of "yours" and "mine." Hence, one needs recognize the requirement for a critical distance that keeps the self from simple absorption in the world of the other. This critical distance in our discourse makes possible a self-affirmation in the dialogic exchange, implicating a subject that refuses domination, subordination, or ideological seduction by the discourse of the other.

In our sketch of the portrait of the subject as questioner thus far we have marked out the contours of embodiment and discourse. The subject as embodied is constituted in and through discourse. This discourse, we have noted, implicates a flesh-and-blood speaker who defines him- or herself through dialogic transactions with other speakers. No longer simply a grammatological function, the subject takes on the lineaments of an engaged rhetor whose traces become discernible in the ongoing affairs of the polis. This marks the move from grammatology to dialogue.

Our recovery of embodiment and discourse sets the stage for a third feature in our sketch of the questioner interrogating her/his status as subject. This third feature is the questioner as agentive subject.

The embodied subject is constituted in and through discourse. It is also constituted in and through action. And this constitution in and through action is no more a sovereign self-constitution than is the constitution of the subject in and through discourse and dialogue. In dealing with the dynamics of action one also needs to recognize vectors proceeding from the other. The actions of the subject are always contextualized in such a manner as to be responsive to some prior action upon it. As the speaking subject is dialogically involved with other speakers, so the agentive subject remains contextualized in its responsivity to action by others upon it. The agentive subject is not a pregiven entity with an impervious self-identity. It is constituted in and through its responses to that which is other than self. Indeed, it is not an entity at all, neither pregiven nor postgiven. It is more like an event that incorporates previous responses in its developing history.

An acknowledgment of the alterity that occasions the constitution of the subject in its responsivity to other subjects does not mean that the subject in its odyssey of self-constitution is somehow at the mercy of the other, caught up within the constraints of heteronomy. The subject of action exercises a *genuine* freedom in the pulsations of embodiment. However, to characterize this genuine freedom, implicated as a seat and source of empowerment within the wider economy of prior and contemporary actors, as "autonomous" is equally misleading. As the acting subject is not constrained by *hetero-nomy*—that is, subordinated to the "law of the other"—so also it is not *auto-nomos*—that is, a "law unto itself." The embodied, speaking, and acting subject cannot be free by itself. Neither autonomy nor heteronomy provide proper determinants of the questioning subject. There is a freedom in being-with-others that is located on the hither side of the either/or of autonomy versus heteronomy, a freedom that remains responsive to the call and actions of the other. The mistake of Sartre was to fail to recognize this expression of freedom. For Sartre the freedom of the subject as *pour-soi* is a pure freedom of self-determination, even in the midst of the encroachments of facticity. Merleau-Ponty corrected Sartre on this issue, and he made the critical point explicit when he wrote: "Subjectivity is not motionless identity with itself: as with time, it is of its essence, to be genuine subjectivity, to open itself to an Other and to go forth from itself."[21]

The acting subject, like the embodied speaking subject, rides the crest of a hermeneutical self-implicature. It is called into being in its deliberating, deciding, and acting. As we took a line from Benveniste in sketching the profile of the speaking subject, "Ego is he who *says* 'ego'," so we borrow a line from Paul Ricoeur in his characterization of the constitution of the agentive subject as a self-recognition proceeding via a "prereflexive imputation of myself" in the act of deciding.[22] The subject is implicated in the throes of decision making. The central point at issue regarding the status of the agentive subject is that decision calls the subject into being as the agent in the project to be undertaken and realized. Ricoeur does well to underscore that the "self-imputation" that is at work here is *prereflexive.* We are not dealing with a cognitive act of theoretical observation in which the self strives to become present to itself via an intricate reflexive duplication. The hermeneutical self-implicature that marks out the trace of an agentive subject is a self-imputation via action rather than a detached observation of a reflexive state of affairs.

It also needs to be underscored that the subject that is implicated and called into being by its deliberation, decision, and action is not an isolated *voluntas solus ipse,* an abiding self-contained, monadic self-identity. Its constitution always proceeds *with the other.* It establishes itself as a genuine agent for change in its consensual and dissensual responses to prior action upon it. The who of action, like the who of discourse, can make a difference in the world of communicative praxis. The implicated actor is the source of empowerment and the agency of enactment. Although neither a metaphysical substance nor an epistemological zero-point origin, the human self as subject can become an agent of social change and cultural transformation. And it is precisely at this juncture that we find the postmodern discourse about the "death of the subject" to come up short, producing a rather profound irony in the postmodern clarion call for *empowerment.* Empowerment by and for whom? we need to ask. And in pursuing this question we will find that the ascription of some notion of agency to the subject is required to account for the entwined phenomena of personal and social history.

Some Concluding Observations

Our sketch of the questioner questioning her/his status as questioning subject has yielded a portrait of three intercalating profiles—the questioner as embodied, as discursive, and as agentive. In the aftermath of the deconstruction of the subject as metaphysical substratum and epistemological foundation we find that talk about the subject as embodied speaking agent continues to be required. The grammars of "subject" and "subjectivity" need not be excised from our philosophical vocabularies so long as one remains vigilant of their delimited significations. We began tracking the profiles of the questioner as subject through a critical engagement with representatives of the linguistic turn from both the Anglo and the Continental traditions of philosophical inquiry. In our critical investigations we recommended a *weiterdenken* with the two traditions, involving more specifically Oxford analysis with its ordinary language approach and the Continental grammatological approach, in the hope of widening the perspectives on the issue at hand.

In a somewhat wider context it would be possible to frame our general project as an effort to think beyond the longstanding dichotomy of empirical and transcendental analysis that has been with us through much of our modern history. A fruitful exploration of the profiles of the deconstructed subject will require avoiding the horns of this peculiar inherited philosophical dilemma. A heightened sensitivity to the inscriptions of the historical in the self-understanding and self-constitution of the subject will forestall being impaled on the transcendental horn of the dilemma. Michel Foucault needs to be credited for having called this to our attention when he writes: "One has to dispense with the constituent subject to arrive at an analysis which can account for the constitution of the subject within a historical framework . . . without having to make reference to a subject which is either transcendental in relation to the field of events or runs in its empty sameness throughout the course of history."[23]

However, after having discovered that the transcendental ego is unable to account for our embodiment and historical inherence, one needs be wary about appeals to an abstract empiricism that pulverizes both the subject and world into discrete and atomistic granules of disassociated data. This appeal to atomism, both in our metaphysical and epistemological inquiries, is an invitation to positivism in philosophy and behaviorism in psychology. We have already noted the behavioristic orientation in Ryle's linguistic turn. Even in the "speech act theory" of latter-day ordinary language philosophy one can detect vestiges of an abstract empiricism in which efforts are made to analyze speaking performances as comprised of separable speech acts, decontextualized from discourse as a communicative endeavor in which meaning is the product of historically situated rhetors and interlocutors. An abstract empiricism appears to infect even the ordinary language approaches to the issues at hand.

So also one can observe infectious strains of an abstract empiricism in a philosophy of action where action is dissected into bits of bodily behavior without due regard to the wider context of an embodied being-in-the-world. Specific acts remain inseparable from the social practices in which they achieve their signification. The embeddedness of acts, both linguistic and behavioral, in historically imbued social practices requires a delimitation of empiricist criteria in addressing matters with the vestiges of a reductionist vocabulary within the isolated and hyperspecialized discipline of "philosophy of action." When the data in this specialized discipline are defined as insular bits of behavior—the raised arm, the knee jerk , the nod, the wink, the smile, and the caress—in isolation from the projects and backgrounds of social practices, the stage is set for a reification of sensory qualities and a splitting off of constitutive elements from the holistic context in which they first achieve sense and significance.

It may well be that the most trustworthy guide for directing us around the sirens of an abstract empiricism on the one hand and an abstract transcendentalism on the other hand is the "Radical Empiricism" as proposed by William James. James had an uncanny knack for describing what he called "the world experienced" without reifying the described contents into insular, nontendential, and self-contained sense data, which he found to be the disconcerting constraints of traditional empiricism. "The world experienced," writes James, "comes at all times with our body as its centre, centre of vision, centre of action, centre of interest."[24]

James here opens a path to the space of the human subject in an experienced world in which the subject is always already contextualized as embodied center of vision, action, and interest. Plainly enough, "experience" remains James's point of departure, and this defines his philosophy as "empiricism." However, the adjective *radical* highlights his empiricism as a more holistic and consistently contextualized approach to experience. The "world experienced" comes to us not as pulverized bits and pieces of isolated and insular perceptual sense data, nor as atomistic bits of abstracted bodily reflexes, but rather it makes its presence felt as a holistic environment as the proper habitat for our vision, action, and interest. It is a world with what James called "fringes," which provide a background horizon with its insinuations of sense and significance. The figurations of our perceptions and actions are always *con*-figured against a ground, both background and foreground, that provides resources for a con-textualized understanding of our being in the world.

We also, however, need to be reminded of James's reservations about transcendental philosophy, which travel with his concerns about abstract empiricism. We do not need, he informs us, a tran-scendental ego to descend from on high to provide the determination of sense in the goings on in the world as experienced. James's critical posture is, if you will, two pronged. It calls into question both tradi-tional empiricism and traditional rationalism, and he chides each for their abstracted viewpoints on the concrete configurations of world experience. After the dust of the excessive intellectualism of tran-scendental philosophy and the pulverization of sense contents in an abstracted empiricism has settled, James is able to locate a vibrant intentionality in our discourse and action as we make our way about in a world of everyday affairs.

In marking out a path between the Scylla of traditional rational-ism and the Charybdis of tradition empiricism, James's radical empiricism invites a conversation with affiliates of another contem-porary philosophical perspective. In James's emphasis on the impor-tance of the grammar of fringes, fields, and horizons we find com-mon cause with voices in the phenomenological tradition. It is well documented that Husserl credited James with helping him find his way out of psychologism and acknowledged him as a veritable genius of concrete phenomenological description.[25] Even more strik-ing similarities come to the fore in a comparison of James's radical empiricism with Maurice Merleau-Ponty's existential phenomenol-ogy. Merleau-Ponty's use of the "figure-ground structure" of percep-tion, which he developed on the basis of his studies in Gestalt psy-chology, recalls James's requirement for attending to fringes and backgrounds in making sense of our lived experience. Also in James's descriptions of the world experienced as presented "at all times with our body as its centre" we see an anticipation of Merleau-Ponty's extensive explorations of the "lived body" *(le corps vécu)* as the place from which perception originates, from which action proceeds, and from which concerns are configured. This is not body viewed as an abstracted Cartesian *res extensa,* a mechanistic juxtaposition of parts, or a soft machine. James and Merleau-Ponty are in agreement that a search for the subject in question will lead neither to an abstracted mental substance nor to an equally abstracted physiological mechanism.[26]

We have traversed some distance in our search for the subject who in recent times has had the very being of his/her subjectivity called into question. We began with some historical observations of the fate of signifiers like "subject," "ego," "self," and "mind" in modern and contemporary philosophy. We made particular note of the declared bankruptcy of these signifiers in the wake of deconstructionist critique. We then consulted the resources of linguistics and discourse analysis, action theory, and the grammar of embodiment in wending our way toward a portrait of the questioner. We have ended with a response to the call for a radical empiricism and an invitation to search for the questioner in the folds of a world experienced in which the comportment of an embodied, speaking, and acting questioner might become visible.

The Recovery of the Phenomenological Subject

In Conversation with Ricoeur, Derrida, and Levinas

THE LEGACY OF PHENOMENOLOGY

IN 1945 MAURICE MERLEAU-PONTY began the preface to his classic work *Phénoménologie de la perception,* with the observation that the reader might find it odd that the question What is phenomenology? still needs to be asked one-half a century after the first writings of Edmund Husserl. The fact however remains, wrote Merleau-Ponty, that this question still awaits an answer. Some fifty years after the publication of Merleau-Ponty's seminal work on perception we are still asking the question What is phenomenology? To be sure, we are now asking this question against the backdrop of the bountiful legacy of phenomenological inquiry from Husserl to Heidegger and from Sartre to Merleau-Ponty, and quite beyond them all—but we are still asking the question.

This golden era of phenomenological discourse during the twentieth century provided numerous critical analyses and commentaries on contesting claims for *transcendental* phenomenology, *existential* phenomenology, and *hermeneutical* phenomenology. At certain junctures these claims converged; at other times they remained quite at odds with each other. However, among the participants in the philosophical forays that enlivened the conversations one was able to detect an agreement that the abiding requirement of philosophy is to return to the phenomena themselves. In this there was of course a recollection of the original site of Husserl's contribution in his call *"zu den Sachen selbst!"* even though quite clearly differences as to what comprised the *Sachen,* and how one is to effect a return to them, were voiced across the phenomenological landscape.

For those of you here assembled in the halls of this world-class university, I do not have to rehearse the history of these rather remarkable developments. You are very familiar with them all. I need only to highlight the specific features of the phenomenological movement that make up the background for my conversation with you today. These have to do with the role of the subject in the early and later writings of Husserl; the introduction of the *Existenz*-problem by Heidegger; and the legacies of Husserl and Heidegger in the philosophies of Sartre and Merleau-Ponty. This will then provide us with a philosophical landscape for addressing the assaults on the subject and the structures of subjectivity in the poststructuralist mindset. It is in the poststructuralist/deconstructionist/postmodern literature that we find the most aggressive delimitation of the grammars of subject and subjectivity.

That which provides the binding textuality in the development from the early to the later writings of Husserl is a shift from the requirement for attending to the data themselves to the call for a return to the lifeworld *(Rückgang auf die Lebenswelt).* The story of the subject that is told in this shift is one in which the central character unfolds from an epistemologically centered *ego-cogito* to a praxis-oriented world-experiencing life *(welt-erfahrendes Leben),* with the accompanying move from a disembodied act-intentionality to a more existentially oriented and embodied functioning intentionality *(fungierende Intentionalität).* It was thus that Husserl in his own way was able to raise the *Existenz*-problem that was later in different ways taken up by Heidegger, Sartre, and Merleau-Ponty.

When the *ego-cogito* is animated and vitalized in the guise of a *Dasein,* a *pour-soi,* or a *corps vécu,* the being and behavior of the subject undergoes a significant refiguration. The tired ancient and modern well-worn exercises of founding a self-subsisting monadic subject and stable epistemological zero-point origin become profoundly delimited. Yet, plainly enough, one has not displaced the subject in every sense conceivable. The repeated pronouncements of the demise of the subject and the death of the author, echoes of which can still clearly be heard today, may indeed be requiems that are somewhat premature and overly exaggerated.

The current republic of philosophy is in need of a recovery of the phenomenological subject. This is a particularly urgent requirement in the aftermath of the displacement of the subject by the more radical versions of deconstructionist and postmodernist thought. Although in agreement with the proponents of deconstruction that too much capital has been invested in the metaphysical subject of the ancients and the epistemological subject of the moderns, I wish to discuss with you today the proposal that a dismantling of the traditional metaphysical and epistemological foundations for subjectivity does not lead to a displacement of the subject per se. Although we will allow for a grammar of *replacement*, we have profound worries about a wholesale *displacement* of the subject, either in the guise of author, speaker, or agent of action. Out general argument is that the deconstruction of traditional metaphysics and epistemology as providing support for projects of self-understanding and self-constitution opens up a fresh philosophical landscape, which provides an opportunity for the exploration of a new space of subjectivity in which traces of a phenomenological subject remain intact.

The portrait of the phenomenological subject that we will sketch is admittedly significantly refigured. It is no longer a portrait of a universal and disembodied transcendental ego, abstracted from the concrete discursive and cultural practices that make up the fabric of human life. This new figuration makes room for the effects of language and social institutions in its very constitution. The recovered phenomenological subject is a speaking, acting, embodied, and thoroughly socialized subject that remains irreducible to any of its manifold functions and attributes. The principal phenomenological feature that continues to characterize the subject in the aftermath of its deconstruction as metaphysical substrate and epistemological foundation is its *responsivity within the dynamics of experience.* It is for this reason that we consider it important to recall the emphasis that the later Husserl placed on the notion of "world-experiencing life" and its functioning intentionality in its everyday, praxis-oriented world-existence. As world-experiencing life, the phenomenological subject is textured by its lived-through responses to prior discourse and prior action upon it. The economy of this world-experiencing subject, and particularly vis-a-vis its ethical expression, is stimulated by what we have come to call "the ethic of the fitting response."

Our project of recovering a world-experiencing phenomenological subject, oriented toward ethical responsivity, takes shape as a conversation with three illustrious contemporary French philosophers on three related aspects of our current topic. We will solicit the contributions of Paul Ricoeur in exploring the profile of the subject as agent in our extended sketch of the self as subject. An engagement with Jacques Derrida will provide the occasion for addressing the discursive subject, and particularly as it augers its way to "responsibility." And our reflections on the ethical subject will call upon the contributions of Emmanuel Levinas.

RICOEUR AND THE ACTING SUBJECT

It is difficult to exaggerate the contributions of Paul Ricoeur to the development of twentieth-century phenomenology. Herbert Spiegelberg refers to Ricoeur in his massive two-volume *The Phenomenological Movement* as "the best informed French historian of phenomenology."[27] This laudatory assessment is certainly well deserved. However, it requires a further elaboration. Not only is Ricoeur an eminent historian of phenomenology, he has fashioned a quite distinctive philosophical approach of his own in responding to the phenomenological classics of the twentieth century. Even in the work which may well be his most explicitly historical account of Edmund Husserrl's contribution, *Husserl: An Analysis of His Phenomenology*, he integrates his seven studies of the main topics in Husserl's philosophy with his own take on the issues at stake. This becomes particularly evident in the seventh study in the work, "Methods and Tasks of a Phenomenology of the Will," in which he provides a critical linkage of Husserl's achievements on the topic with his own existential and hermeneutical approach to the issues.[28]

It is precisely this investigation of the method and governing concepts in a phenomenology of the will that takes center stage in Ricoeur's monumental study, *Freedom and Nature: The Voluntary and the Involuntary*—a work that first appeared in Paris in 1950 as the first volume of a projected three-volume *La Philosophie de la volonté.* In this work the structure and dynamics of willing is investigated with a painstaking precision within the parameters of a descriptive phenomenology. The method is one of eidetic analysis, indicating a quite significant indebtedness to Husserl as the father of transcendental and eidetic phenomenology. But already in this first volume of the projected lengthier project we see intimations of a broadening of the phenomenological program to include existential and hermeneutical considerations.

The eidetic structure of the will encompasses two critical moments. There is the structure of motive and decision and the structure of action and movement. Plainly enough these two moments overlap in the odyssey of life as an entwinement of the voluntary and the involuntary. There are no decisions without motives, indicating the role of the involuntary; the play of motives with their constitutive needs and desires confer upon decision a continuity with the involuntary. But motives acquire direction only when appropriated by the will in the act of deciding, and it is in this appropriation that we can discern the intimate dialectic of the voluntary and the involuntary. We also see the workings of this dialectic in the second moment within the eidetic structure of the will. Decision entails the possibility and dynamic of action. Action is thus understood as the projection of willing in such a wise that it effects a change in the world. It soon becomes evident that with Ricoeur's analysis one quickly moves beyond the traditional and barren problematic of free will versus determinism, which belies a mistaken acceptance of a sharp dichotomy of the voluntary pitted against the involuntary.

Within the throes of the dynamic of willing (with its constitutive features of motive, decision, action, and movement), we are able to track Ricoeur's recovery of a phenomenological subject—not an abiding, monadic substratum, securely positioned beyond the ravages of time and change, but rather a subject constituted and defined by its volitional projects. Ricoeur tracks the genealogy of the phenomenological subject back to a "prereflexive imputation of myself" in the act of deciding. The phenomenological subject is constituted in the agony and ecstasy of decision making. "*Je me decide* . . . , reads the French. *Ich enscheide mich* . . . reads the German. Somewhat cumbersomely rendered into English, we have "I make up my mind" in the act of deciding. In deciding, against the background of my conditioning motives and the foreground of my projected actions, I constitute myself as agentive subject.[29]

In this self-constitution of the self as deciding and acting subject, the voluntary and the involuntary, freedom and nature, are delivered from their longstanding and unacceptable dichotomies. However, it needs to be underscored that the freedom that is secured through an eidetic analysis remains a *finite* freedom, situated within a time and space of conflictual motives and contrariant drives, and the actor within the projects of her/his action always acts on the basis of incomplete knowledge and existential risks. It was principally these considerations that pointed the way to a sketching of an empirics of the will in Ricouer's *Fallible Man,* which was designed as a sequel to the eidetics of the will in *Freedom and Nature.*

Ricoeur's contributions toward a recovery of the subject in its agentic mode continue to register in some of his later works. Specifically, in his more recent work, *Oneself as Another,* he points out the limitations of a semantics of action that is unable to locate the agent of the action. What is required is a move from action to agent. A decontextualized conceptual analysis of action stands in danger of atomizing action into "action chains" to the neglect of "the unifying principle that makes these action-chains into higher order practical units."[30] Actions need to be contextualized within the broader space of "practical units," which one might refer to as a web of social practices. Here Ricoeur recognizes clearly enough the requirement to move from an agentless semantics of action to a self-referential ascription of an agent within an economy of social practices.

The continuation of our conversation with Ricoeur pivots quite specifically around his recognition of the need to move beyond an eidetic phenomenology in addressing the recovery of the phenomenological subject for our time. Ricoeur is able to move through the winding corridors of transcendental, existential, and hermeneutical phenomenology with both ease and a depth of comprehension. In the spirit of a collaborative understanding we wish to pursue with him two points regarding the issue at hand. One has to do with nudging his eidetic analysis of a "prereflexive imputation of myself" in the direction of what I have come to call "hermeneutical self-implicature," and the other involves an expansion of his notion of "practical units" via an analysis of this notion into a configuration of "communicative praxis." At issue here is the request for a more explicit situating of the agentive subject within a dynamic of hermeneutical self-constitution and within the wider context of praxis as a communicative endeavor.

These are issues that I have examined in my own *Communicative Praxis and the Space of Subjectivity*—a project that I understand to be quite complementary to Ricoeur's achievements on related topics.[31]

DERRIDA AND THE SHIFT FROM THE
GRAMMATOLOGICAL SUBJECT TO THE
SUBJECT AS RESPONSIBILITY

Derrida's role in the recovery of the phenomenological subject is less pronounced and more nuanced than is the case in the philosophy of Ricoeur. But even in Derrida's most direct assault on Husserl's philosophical program an acknowledgment of the resources for phenomenological description becomes evident. To be sure, any uses of phenomenology need to be pruned of their transcendental and eidetic construction—"deconstructed," if you will—but the task of pursuing the sense of that which shows itself as the primary task of phenomenology remains in place. This is evident even in the frontal attack on Husserl's doctrine of representation *(Vergegenwärtigung)* by Derrida in *Speech and Phenomena*. In this essay, Husserl's doctrine of the ego-cogito as the seat of representational knowledge is profoundly problematized by way of a sustained critique of the concept of "presence." Knowledge as *re*-presentation is charged with the task of recalling a former presence constituted as an invariant and atemporal ideal—as a *noema* or *cogitatum* ripe for prehension by a constituting *noesis* or *cogito*.

The principal problem that Derrida finds with this construct of representational knowledge, with its egological foundation, is that the presence that is allegedly recollected in an act of re-presentation is infected with a grammatological indeterminacy of convertible signifiers and signifieds. If there is no determinate presence to be recalled, then the task of re-presentation appears to become moot. However, dismantling the constructs of representational knowledge with its supporting egology does not entail a displacement of all discourse concerning matters of the subject.

Derrida appears to be quite clear about that in his classic reply to Serge Doubrovsky at the much publicized international symposium on "The Languages of Criticism and the Sciences of Man," held at Johns Hopkins University in 1966.

First of all, I didn't say that there was no center, that we could get along without the center. I believe that the center is a function, not a being—a reality, but a function. And this function is absolutely indispensable. I don't destroy the subject. I situate it. That is to say, I believe that at a certain level both of experience and of philosophical and scientific discourse one can not get along without the notion of subject. It is a question of knowing where it comes from and how it functions.[32]

Now to speak of the center, the subject as centered, as a function—and one that is indeed indispensable—invites some clarification on the meaning of "function." It is a long-established habit of thought to think of a function as always being a function *of something*—either an underlying substrate or a formal structure. The former use of function is present in the traditional substance/function distinction; the latter is exemplified in the structure/function polarity of structuralism. But surely neither of these distinctions can find a happy home in Derrida's deconstructionist project. They would simply catapult us back into either a metaphysics of presence or a formalism of structuralist science—and it is precisely from these that Derrida has sought to deliver us.

But what meaning then are we to ascribe to Derrida's spin on "function"? It would seem that here one would need to speak of a *grammatological* function, which situates the subject as a function of discourse, and more specifically as a function of *écriture*, a coefficient of textuality. Admittedly, the subject that is implicated in such a function is existentially deprived. A subject thusly situated is thin and bloodless; and it is well known that Derrida has received a fair amount of criticism on this matter, suffering the accusation of trafficking in pantextualism. Now this accusation might hold some merit were one to take his reply to Doubrovsky as his final statement on the issue. But more recently we have learned that such is not the case.

At the conference dealing with the topic "Who comes after the subject?" twenty years after the Johns Hopkins symposium, Derrida was asked a question by Jean-Luc Nancy similar to the one that was posed by Doubrovsky at the earlier gathering. Nancy framed his question along the lines of an inquiry into a possible "who" that might still sustain our interest after the grammar of the subject appears to have outworn its usefulness. Derrida's reply is measured and insightful.

What are we aiming at in the deconstructions of the "subject" when we ask ourselves what, in the structure of the classical subject, continues to be required by the question "Who?" . . . I would add something that remains required by both the definition of the classical subject and by these latter nonclassical motifs, namely, a certain *responsibility*. The singularity of the "who" is not the individuality of a thing that would be identical to itself, it is not an atom. It is a singularity that dislocates or divides itself in gathering itself together to answer to the other, whose call somehow precedes its own identification with itself.[33]

Of particular import in Derrida's response to Nancy's query is his emphasis on the subject as *responsibility*, as respondent to the call of the other. Here we find a clear indication that there is indeed life of the subject after the demise of its classical alleged metaphysical criteria of self-identity. The 'who" is not a thing that would be identical to itself. The "who" is an answer to a call that antedates its own identification with itself.

How does one account for this shift, a Heideggerlike *Kehre*, in the thought of Derrida from the subject as grammatological function to the subject as responsibility? Explanations of shifting textual strategies and sliding topical foci in the intellectual odyssey of an author are never easy to come by. And such may indeed be the case in Derrida's own somewhat surprising change of venue in his own philosophical development. Nonetheless, we are disposed to offer some suggestions as to how this move in perspectives on the subject comes about.

The first point that needs to be made, and indeed underscored, is that Derrida's *Kehre*, like that of Heidegger's shift from the question as to the *meaning* of being to that of the *truth* of being, should not be understood as a brute discontinuity in which the earlier perspective is repudiated by the latter. What is at issue is more like a play with hermeneutical profiles so as to get a better bead on the phenomenon at issue—in full recognition of course that there can be no foundational and incorrigible tragectory that delivers the identity of the subject in question.

Now there is a wider consideration that comes into play at this juncture, and one that returns us to our lead-off question regarding the *phenomenological* recovery of the subject. Can one still find phenomenological insinuations in Derrida's *Kehre,* which allegedly moves within the constraints of a deconstructive strategy? The answer to this question, I think, needs to be a positive one. Although somewhat tenuous, connections with the Husserlian phenomenological project remain intact—and particularly when we recall Husserl's own *Kehre* in his shift from his early period of phenomenological inquiry as guided by the mandate "to the data themselves" to the later period of *The Crisis of European Sciences and Transcendental Phenomenology* in which the principal directive is a "return to the lifeworld." Derrida recognizes the importance of this shift in the thought of Husserl in his observation that "when, in the period of the *Crisis,* history breaks through into phenomenology, a new space of questioning is opened, one that will be difficult to maintain in the regional limits which were so long prescribed for it."[34] The guiding thematic of the *Crisis,* requiring a return to the lifeworld, opens up a new space of inquiry on the fortunes of the phenomenological subject. The subject, as Derrida indicates, undergoes a descent into history, and in this descent into history one encounters the requirement for a subject in the guise of "the singularity of the 'who'" that is properly named *responsibility* in its response to the call of the other.

The lesson about the ways of deconstruction to be learned from all this finds its analogy in what Merleau-Ponty defined as the lesson to be learned from Husserl's phenomenological reduction. The truth of the reduction, Merelau-Ponty informed us, is that no complete reduction is possible. Might what is said of the method of reduction also be said of the strategy of deconstruction? The lifeworld with its world-experiencing subject remains in the brackets while the reduction is in process. The "who" that is reclaimed after the classical and neoclassical definitions of the subject have outworn their usefulness continues to make its presence felt during the varied deconstructive maneuvers.

It is the return to the lifeworld thematic that provides the wider context for explaining Derrida's shift in his telling of the fortunes and misfortunes of the subject. There is, however, a more local context of considerations at issue. It is apparent to the discerning reader that the grammar of responsibility, which takes center stage in Derrida's move from investigations of grammatological functions to questions about the "who," belies a strain of indebtedness to his former mentor, who himself has played a major role in shaping the directions of current French philosophy—Emmanuel Levinas.

LEVINAS ON ALTERITY AND THE ETHICAL SUBJECT

Levinas, like Derrida, begins his philosophical journey with a respectful critique of Husserlian phenomenology. In his masterful work *Théorie de l'intuition dans la phénoménologie de Husserl*, Levinas brings into conceptual clarity the central issues that were at stake in Husserl's celebrated doctrine of the intuition of essences *(Wesenschau)*. To be sure, in the end he reproaches Husserl for his intellectualism in sacrificing the concrete and vague world of perception to eidetic determinants (and recommends a shift to Heidegger's existential phenomenology with its depiction of being as a center of action and a field of concern); nonetheless, his admiration for the accomplishments of Husserl are clearly evident.

According to Levinas, the principal adjustment in Husserl's thought that is required, vis-a-vis the issue of the status of the subject, is an explication that the sense of the other as an *other* self is not simply the result of an act of constitution within the eidetic structure of transcendental subjectivity. This does not mean, however, that Husserl's project of a transcendental reduction is simply to be abandoned. Levinas is quite clear about that. Indeed, Levinas voices his approval of Husserl's project when he writes: "Husserl's transcendental reduction has, as its vocation, to awaken the I from numbness, to reanimate its life and its horizons lost in anonymity."[35] This bold project of awakening and reanimating calls upon the resources of an intersubjective reduction, which Husserl carries through in the "Fifth Meditation" of his *Cartesian Meditations*. In a telling summation, Levinas expresses the point as follows: "The intersubjective reduction, starting from the other *(l'autre),* will tear the I out of its coincidence with self and with the center of the world, even if Husserl never ceases, for all that, to think about the relationship between me and the other in terms of knowledge."[36] Husserl saw clearly enough the need to acknowledge the impingement of the other within the structure of transcendental intersubjectivity. However, he was unable to move beyond the strictures of thinking of the relationship between self and other as a determination of "knowledge." And clearly here we are to understand knowledge along the lines of a representational theory of knowledge that issues from a self-identical ego as epistemological foundation.

What is required is a move beyond an epistemological recovery of the self/other relationship, and this move is facilitated through a move to the ethical sphere. Repeatedly we are told by Levinas that ethics is older than epistemology. It is also older than ontology, antedating the Heideggerian *Seinsfrage*. And it is in the domain of ethics that any recovery of the subject is to be sought. For it is only the ethical relation, with its primacy of the face and call of the other, in an accentuated alterity summoning me to respond, that the subject can be awakened from its numbness and reanimated out of its anonymity. The Levinasian accent on a robust alterity becomes at this juncture fully visible. The birth of self-awareness, which is always accompanied by a sense of responsibility, is consequent to the intrusion of the other. We are here clearly outside the bounds of a Hegelian reciprocity of self and other enroute to a mutual acknowledgment. Reciprocity is subordinated to an asymmetry that favors the other.

Concluding Remarks

Our conversation with the three stalwarts of recent French philosophy on the recovery of the phenomenological subject has ushered us onto the terrain of ethics. Ricoeur's phenomenological investigations of the agentive subject as defined by its social practices and Derrida's deconstructive odyssey from the grammatological subject to the subject as responsibility have opened up an inquiry into the relevance and role of the ethical. We have seen how Levinas has staked out the region of the ethical with claims of alterity and asymmetry. Coming to a stand on the terrain of ethics, the phenomenological subject achieves its identity (which is more like what Ricoeur has named *ipse* as contrasted with *idem* identity) by responding to the voice and the visage of the other, who is never simply an alter-ego constituted within the space of an intersubjective reduction. The phenomenological subject advances to its maturity as ethical subject.

We now continue the conversation with Levinas on the role of the ethical in our quest for the phenomenological subject. In a previous work, *Communicative Praxis and the Space of Subjectivity,* to which we have already referred, we traced the genealogy of subjectivity to a responding center at the intersection of ethics and rhetoric, making use of the Greek concept of *kathakonta* to guide our investigations. We came upon the notion of "the fitting response" as indicative of the ethical requirement in the dynamics of communicative praxis. Ethical responsibility, as the performance of the fitting response, is saying and doing that which is fitting within the inter-texualized voices and contextualized practices occurent within the polis. Such a fitting response is always a response to *prior* discourse and action. The ethical requirement of the discursive and agentive subject is to respond in a fitting manner to the discourse and action that always predates its self-constitution.[37]

A lesson to be drawn from our quadrilateral conversation on the story of the phenomenological subject is that any future phenomenology will indeed need to take account of the Levinasian accent on alterity. In doing so one will become aware of the necessity to decenter the interiority of transcendental subjectivity within the bounds of classical phenomenology. This is the first moment in the move to a viable reconfiguration of the phenomenological subject. But there is a second moment, designed to provide a sheet anchor against the tendency to a heteronomy that issues from an unnameable and absolute exteriority. The interiority/exteriority dyad, that informs the tired dichotomy of autonomy versus heteronomy, itself needs to be overcome. In reclaiming the ethical substance of the phenomenological subject we will need to impose quite stringent limitations on the grammar of autonomy and heteronomy as directive for ethical inquiry. In discourse and action answering to the call for a fitting response, it is neither ruminations on the interiority of a "law" that is "my own" *(auto-nomos)* nor appeals to an exteriority of a "law" that comes from "the other" *(hetero-nomos)* that will provide the content and measure of that which is fitting for the requirement for responsibility within the ethos of our civil societies. The content and measure of our ethical dwelling within the economies of our societal claims on rights, duties, and ends invites a transgression of the very notion of a *nomos* of the *eikos,* be it that of an interior law of self-legislation or an exterior law of external subjugation.

Let us suppose that in pursuing the selected topic one were to proceed by way of an appeal to analogies of experience in which the seeing, hearing, acknowledging, assenting, and attesting that involves that which is other gathers a variety of senses across the economy of the experiencing of objects perceived, works of art appreciated, texts interpreted, persons encountered, and alien cultures evaluated. All this testifies to the experience of that which is other, but in such a manner that the reality at issue cannot be reduced to the experiencing itself, imprisoned in a web of subjectivity that determines every experience of the other as an experience of the *other-for-me.* The analogies of experiencing alterity, whatever its range and intensity, invoke a recognition of an incursion of the other that disrupts all facile symmetries of self and other. The other is always already there when the dynamic play of experience is installed. I do not create the other; I respond to that which is other. The perceived house solicits my experience of the house-as-being-perceived; Picasso's *Guernica* sets forth conditions for an aesthetic assessment; a text by Kant challenges my project of interpretation; the facticity of the stranger-at-the-door antedates the experience of stranger-for-me; and the folkways and mores of an alien culture are thrust upon me occasioning ethical evaluations.

It is thus that analogies of experience are able to testify to the incursion of that which is other without assimilating the other into simply another structure of subjectivity—subjectivity with an inter-subjective modality. And such, as Levinas instructs us, is particularly the case when the life of the ethical subject is at issue. In dealing with analogies of experience in regard to the ethical we need to give par-ticular attention to the limitations of classical phenomenology that unwittingly, perhaps, aligned itself with a metaphysics of subjectivity and an epistemology of the primacy of consciousness. Such a delim-itation of classical phenomenology need not, however, entail a jetti-soning of phenomenology as a postmetaphysical elucidation of expe-rience. And it is our contention that the peril in jettisoning such a phenomenology of experience is that the other, who is indeed the ini-tiator of our ethical experience, could neither be seen nor heard.

ESSAY IV

Postmodernism as a
Problem for Metaphysics

IT WOULD SURELY BE a serious omission on my part were I to begin my remarks today without expressing a deeply felt gratitude to the Institute of Human Studies of the Russian Academy of Sciences, and more specifically to Professor Tatiana Artemieva, for the invitation to address the members and guests of the Russian Metaphysical Society. It gives me great pleasure to be a part of the proceedings of this august philosophical gathering.

As we are assembled in this historic and culturally rich city of Saint Petersburg, I find myself having to deal with a quite profound challenge. I have been asked to speak on the subject of metaphysics in the city that gave to the world the genius of a Dostoevsky, who throughout my own professional career has intermittently provided thought-provoking inspiration. Admittedly, Dostoevsky was very modest about his philosophical achievements, noting in his correspondence that although he was rather weak in philosophy his love for philosophy remained very strong; and in one of his many letters to his brother he asks that he send him Kant's *Critique of Pure Reason,* and then adds " "be sure to send Hegel—but particularly Hegel's *History of Philosophy.* Upon that depends my whole future."[38]

Although Dostoevsky continued to be markedly self-effacing in regard to his philosophical talents, one of the better known biographers and interpreters of his life and thought, Nicholas Berdyaev, presents him as "Russia's greatest metaphysician."[39] This assessment

51

of the life and works of Dostoevsky has been endorsed by André Gide in his own intellectual biography of this world-class figure. Gide credits Dostoevsky with having built up through the soul-wrenching questioning by the characters in his sundry novels "an entire system of metaphysics, containing Nietzsche in embryo."[40] The reference to Nietzsche in this context is not incidental, which becomes apparent when we recall Nietzsche's own panegyric on Dostoevsky as "the only psychologist, by the way, from whom I learned something."[41] And here it is important to remember that for Nietzsche "psychology" has as its proper subject matter an exploration of the dynamics of the human soul. As Dostoevsky was able to penetrate the soul of Russia, so Nietzsche was able to comprehend the palpitating and oft-turbulent dynamics of the soul of Dostoevsky.

If we now add to the assessments of Dostoevsky's wider cultural contributions by the likes of Nietzsche, Berdyaev, and Gide the more recent celebration of him by Emmanuel Levinas, we have indeed before us an ecumenical recognition of Dostoevsky's impact on the intellectual life of the twentieth century. In his book *Outside the Subject,* Levinas invites us to recall "the profound truth of Dostoevsky's *Brothers Karamazov,*" and the passage that he has in mind is the often quoted announcement by the saintly and ethically sensitive Alyosha: "We are all guilty of everything and everyone, towards everyone, and I more so than all the others."[42] It is the burden of responsibility in awareness of a universal being-guilty that Alyosha calls to our attention, and it is this burden that comes to mind in the Levinasian meeting of the face of the other—the stranger, the widow, the orphan, the insulted, and the injured—that sets the tone for Levinas's own peculiar metaphysics of alterity and responsibility.

So how does it stand with metaphysics as we enter a new millennium in the wake of a two-thousand-year history of variegated voices on the fortunes and misfortunes of the metaphysical enterprise? The lessons to be learned from this complex and convoluted history are not that easy to sort out. But we are forced to ask the question about the fate of metaphysics for our present age. More specifically, we are called upon to respond to the conjoined questions What is the destiny of metaphysics in our postmodern world and where does one begin in the pursuit of an answer to the question regarding the relevance of metaphysics for our present and our future? Plainly enough, one can never begin at a virginal and pristine beginning. When one makes an effort to begin, one quickly finds that one is always already begun. There are no absolute and untrammeled starting points. Starting points are always contingent and conditional. But one must begin somewhere. So we shall begin with an investigation of the metaphysical fallout from the deconstructive turn in the current philosophical situation of our time.

THE DECONSTRUCTIVE TURN

Quite aware that one can never begin at the beginning because one's situatedness is that of being always already begun, we place ourselves into an ongoing conversation about the effects of deconstruction on the nature and destiny of metaphysical thought. The strategy of deconstruction is one of the principal features of what commonly flies under the flag of "postmodernism." Among the names of the progenitors of postmodern thought, that of Nietzsche, who learned so much about the human condition from Dostoevsky, is given a prominent inscription. In his early work *On Truth and Lies in a Nonmoral Sense,* it is specifically Nietzsche's strategy of *Verstellung* (dissimulation), wherewith to accomplish a deconstruction of *Vorstellung* (representation), that supplies the marker of a postmodern dismantling of foundationalist epistemology. In his later writings the postmodern critique of foundationalist ethics comes to the fore in his heavily accented notion of the transvaluation of all values *(Umwertung alle Werte).* In these bold thought experiments it would indeed seem that Nietzsche set the requirements for a deconstructive turn.

Within more recent decades, however, it was Martin Heidegger and his quite influential left-wing interpreter, Jacques Derrida, who have gained the headlines in the postmodern news of the day. Already in his monumental *Being and Time,* Heidegger proposed a "destruction" *(Destrucktion)* of the history of ontology as metaphysics; and in his companion work, *The Basic Problems of Phenomenology,* he defined his project of destruction as proceeding via a strategy of "deconstruction" *(Abbau).* This strategy was designed to proceed via a dismantling of the categorial framework of traditional metaphysics. It is important, however, not to confuse Heidegger's destruction/deconstruction of traditional metaphysics with the "elimination" of metaphysics as proposed specifically by mid-twentieth-century positivism. Deconstruction does not entail a relegation of metaphysics to the dust bin of philosophical nonsense, as proponents of the positivist persuasion had maintained. It is understood rather as a dismantling of metaphysical conceptual schemes and categories for the purpose of retrieving their originative meaning and relevance. Deconstruction for Heidegger remains a project of deconstructive *retrieval.*

Now it is precisely at this juncture that Heidegger and his illustrious student Derrida part company. Derrida buys into Heidegger's notion of deconstruction but he signs off on his notion of retrieval. The very content of that which is to be retrieved in the wake of a Heideggerian deconstruction of classical and modern metaphysics, namely a reclaimed understanding of Being in terms of a refigured notion of presence, becomes profoundly problematized. It is precisely such a reclamation of the understanding of Being that needs to be brought into question, according to Derrida. For Derrida and company, Heidegger's project falls short of reaching its intended goal and simply culminates in a refurbished metaphysics of presence.

Derrida's strategy, and that of the left-wing Heideggerians more generally, is designed to complete Heidegger's original project of "overcoming" metaphysics by problematizing the very notion of Being as presence. It is basically this strategy, coupled with an attack on logocentrism and a celebration of difference, that defines the philosophical interest of postmodernism and comprises its antimetaphysical thrust. If one were to provide a one-liner describing the misfortunes of metaphysics from a postmodern perspective, one would need to highlight the interrelated themes or topics of logocentrism, difference, and presence.

Against Logocentrism

The much discussed attack on logocentrism by the postmoderns has been waged basically on two fronts. One of the targets is the classical logos doctrine, which clearly is heavily imbued with metaphysical interests. The other target is the modern epistemological paradigm with its heavy investments in methodology and criteriology, producing a state of affairs in which a modal logic with its matrices of quantification and predicate calculus replaces the logos doctrine of the ancients and the medievals.

The classical doctrine of the logos was announced at the dawn of Western philosophy. The very definition of philosophy in the minds of the ancients hinged on the meaning and use of the logos. Hans-Georg Gadamer, both an eminent Plato scholar and sympathetic student of Heidegger, characterizes the traditional logos doctrine as "the grand hypothesis of Greek philosophy" in which rationality is "not first and foremost a property of human self-consciousness but of being itself," whereby "human reason is far more appropriately thought of as part of this rationality instead of as the self-consciousness that knows itself over against an external reality."[43] Plainly enough, the Greeks elevated the logos to a position of preeminence. The portrait of the logos was drawn against the backdrop of specific metaphysical and epistemological presuppositions and claims, involving principally the distinction between the sensible and the intelligible world and the corresponding distinction between opinion and reason. The faculty of reason, in the Greek extolling of the structure and the dynamics of the logos, was deemed to have the resources to apprehend the veritable structure of the intelligible world, the world of rigorous being, which conferred order and direction upon the sensible world of becoming. The logos was seen to function as at once a metaphysical principle and an epistemological determinant.

In the period of modern metaphysics, inaugurated by the epistemological turn within the philosophy of Descartes, the logos doctrine functioned principally as a founding principle for theory of knowledge. This led to a close association, and at times virtual identity, of logos and logic. The *logos* of the *epistēmē,* within the designs of the newly liberated discipline of epistemology, supplies the foundation for a rational reconstruction of the transaction that takes place in the achievement of knowledge—a reconstruction that follows the route of retrieving representational contents. The grand hypothesis of Greek metaphysics, in which the logos was proffered as a determinant of being itself, is replaced with an epistemological construal of the logos as a structure of the human mind. This was given one of its more dominant expressions in Kant's doctrine of the transcendental unity of apperception. Yet, in both the classical metaphysical and modern epistemological accounts of the logos, claims for universality, necessity, and unity remained in force. Apodicity, set in place as the unimpeachable criterion for reliable knowledge, required judgments that were at once universal (always the case) and necessary (unavoidably the case). The traditional oppositions of the universal versus the particular, the necessary versus the contingent, and unity versus plurality, were accepted as a *donnée,* and a rather pronounced optimism regarding the resources of rationality to apprehend that which is universal, necessary, and unified became prevalent. This quickly defined the mindset of modernity, with its obsession with criteriology, rules of method, and representational theories of knowledge.

It is at this juncture that the postmodern challenge registers its most decisive effects. And it does so in its assault on what it considers the overvalued claims of a reason that valorizes universality, necessity, and unity at the expense of an acknowledgment of the realities of particularity, contingency, difference, plurality, and incommensurability. Jean-François Lyotard, one of the more prominent architects of postmodernity, provides us with a consolidation of sorts as to what is at issue in postmodernism when he defines the postmodern as "incredulity toward metanarratives" and as that which "refines our sensitivity to differences and reinforces our ability to tolerate the incommensurable."[44]

Combining the contributions of Heidegger, Derrida, and Lyotard we are now in position to consolidate the general thrust of postmodernism as a philosophical expression. Reacting against the logocentrism of both the ancients and the moderns, it assumes the posture of a discourse on the related notions of deconstruction and difference, bringing to the fore the vagaries of being as presence, leading to a combined dismanteling of the presence of the object and the presence of the subject. It is against the backdrop of these interwoven notions and motifs that the postmodern challenge garners its most formidable confrontation with the enterprise of metaphysics.

THE CELEBRATION OF DIFFERENCE

The use of the vocabulary of difference is not an event of recent date. It extends far back into the history of philosophy both East and West. In the annals of Western thought the notion of difference received one of its earliest articulations in the philosophy of Plato. As is well known, it is in his dialogue *Sophist* that Plato delineates the topography of the world of forms in such a way that being, sameness, difference, motion, and rest fall out as exemplars of the "greatest kinds." What we learn from the schematization of the greatest kinds of forms is that some of them blend with each other while others do not. Being, sameness, and difference happily combine or blend one with another. Motion and rest, however, although they do indeed partake of being, sameness, and difference, plainly enough cannot blend with each other. To be sure, both motion and rest have a status in being, and each partakes of sameness in that each is identical with itself, and each blends with difference in that the one is different from the other. But to assert that they blend with each other would land us in a blatant contradiction.

The lesson that we are taught from this recognition that some of the greatest kinds combine and others do not is that in the world of forms there are natural cleavages or joints, and that one will quickly fall into error if one tries to combine lesser forms (e.g., forms of natural kinds and artifacts) that do not fit the ontologically secured cleavages. One would be very much mistaken, for example, if one combined the form "quadruped" with the form "feathered." On the basis of this ontologically anchored theory of knowledge, Plato was able to respond to the Sophists' claim that it is impossible to make a false statement. One can indeed think and say what is not the case. But thinking that which *is not* does not reduce to having nothing at all before the mind. It means rather having the wrong form before the mind. It is thus of some importance that one keeps negations—that is, statements of not-being—somehow within the folds of being, lest one catapult into a sea of chaos in which not-being assumes the status of an independent principle. Not-being is *difference from* other entities, a determination of *otherness* rather than the absence of being. But this *difference* or *otherness* remains constitutive of the *sameness* or *identity* of that which is in some sense *present*. Of everything that is, one can predicate a finite number of features that define what it is and an infinite number of features that characterize what it is not. Not-being remains constitutive of being, and as difference or otherness it remains linked to the region of being as presence, and indeed presence in its modality of sameness or identity.

It is this linkage of being as presence with not-being as difference that is brought into question by the representatives of postmodernism. They are of the mind that difference needs be given a more prominent role to play. Derrida, in particular, underscores this point. Difference, attests Derrida, is "'older' than Being itself," and the notion of presence that has traveled with that of Being since the advent of metaphysics "is a determination and effect within a system which is no longer that of presence but that of difference."[45] It is here that the valorization of difference attains its most intensified expression. Difference is accorded a space above presence as sameness or identity, and assumes the function of a principle of all principles.

The elevation of difference to a status above and otherwise than the being of sameness attains a socio-political urgency for combating the logocentrism of a tradition that has always courted ethnocentrism and a phallocentrism as fellow travelers. The "white mythology" of the logocentric tradition has been unable to come to terms with ethnic diversity, as it also was unable to surmount the marginalization of the feminine. Metaphors of ethnic superiority and male dominance permeate the texts of Western metaphysics from the time of its earliest beginnings.[46]

THE GRAMMAR OF PRESENCE

The extolling of difference as exceeding the dignity of being itself has some profound consequences for the classical grammar of presence. The well-honed classical metaphysical concepts of *eidos, ousia, einai, onta,* and *physis* all made bold semantic claims on the notion of "presence." Being, whether in its ontological or ontic modality, stakes out that which is in some sense present. And with this claim upon presence we are confronted with a rather firmly entrenched ambiguity of senses. There is presence in the sense of that which is *given*—presence as the givenness of "being presented"; and there is the sense of presence as a dimension of temporality. This ambiguity, one quickly observes, is orthogonal to the putative levels or orders of being, as well as to the multiple profiles of presentative acts of consciousness.

Within the metaphysical construct of ascending levels or orders of being—what Arthur Lovejoy felicitously named "the great chain of being"—we find claims for the presence of entities from the lowest terrestrial prime matter to the highest celestial reaches of divine being. Within the epistemological register of acts of consciousness, both in the constitution of sense and in the determination of reference, there are overlapping claims for the alleged presentment of sense data, perceived objects, contents of the imagination, and concepts for judgment. Presence as object of knowledge is given in the exercises of perception, imagination, conception, and judgment; and it is given always within a temporal horizon of that which is present now, that which was present in the past, and that which is anticipated to be present in the future.

Within the company of postmoderns it is Derrida in particular who has called our attention to the vagaries of the concept of presence. Deconstructing Husserl's doctrine of representation as a rendering present *(Vergegenwärtigung),* he shows how the present that is to be re-presented suffers the fate of a perpetual deferment. That such is the case ought not be all that surprising given that the original present, that which is to be *re*-presented, escapes determination for want of a present that abides throughout the vicissitudes of temporal passage.[47]

The deconstructive turn thus appears to reach its telos of fulfillment—if indeed the language of fulfillment is appropriate here!—in an aggressive dismantling of all vestiges of a metaphysics of presence. In the aftermath of such a turn there is neither a presence of an object nor the presence of a subject to be set forth. The traditional subject-object vocabulary, so dear to classical and modern metaphysics and epistemology, has been effectively undercut. The signifiers of our grammar in the wake of the deconstructive turn are shorn of any resources for identifying the properly signified, whether such be an object-as-signified or the subject as the source of signification.

Now where does this all leave us in our assessment of the fortunes of metaphysics? Plainly enough, it leaves us not only without reliable criteria for the identity of objects and things. It also leaves us without trustworthy marks for self-identity. Subject and object alike suffer the fate of a devouring evanescence and a perpetual deferring, neither remaining long enough to enjoy an identifiable presence. It were as though in one fell swoop all traditional supports for metaphysical claims have been undercut and the very grammar of the metaphysical vocabulary impugned. If the official requirement for doing metaphysics is to carry out an investigation of the meaning of "being qua being" *(on ē on),* as Aristotle had announced in Book Gamma of his *Metaphysics,* it would seem that this time-honored task has now been abandoned. The operative vocabulary in the economy of metaphysics is regarded as having outworn its usefulness. Talk about the presence of beings, be they objects or subjects, defined by identifying attributes and properties, is considered to be talk bereft of signification.

RESPONDING TO THE CHALLENGE

How does one respond to the challenging announcement of the event of postmodernity with its deconstructive turn, heralding the end of a longstanding metaphysics of presence? Is the deconstruction of the stock categories of traditional metaphysics the end of metaphysics per se, or might one still find resources for the possibility of a metaphysics that is aware of its own delimitations, a minimalist and oblique metaphysics? Let us suppose that such a metaphysics would indeed be possible. Clearly, a delimited and minimalist metaphysics would need to take its point of departure not from cosmological speculations about universality and infinity but rather from an ontology of human finitude. The sketching of such a metaphysics, in response to the postmodern challenge, would require a reconsideration of the dynamics of reason and would need to give particular attention to the role of difference and the fate of presence.

The delimitation of the resources of reason for the metaphysical enterprise is admittedly not an event of recent date. The contributions of Hume's empiricism and Kant's critical rationalism provide two classic illustrations of such a delimitation. In the thought of both of these modern thinkers the soaring wings of traditional metaphysics have been decisively clipped. For Hume, neither relations of reason nor relations pertaining to matters of fact are able to deliver metaphysically grounded knowledge about the world. For Kant, concepts without percepts are empty, as percepts without concepts are congenitally blind, and all efforts on the part of pure reason to surmount its finitude lands one in paralogisms, antinomies, and transcendental illusions.

Yet, for all of their efforts in delimiting the resources of reason, Hume's skeptical empiricism and Kant's critical rationalism continued to traffic in abstracted epistemic presuppositions that courted claims for problematic notions of presence. Hume's doctrine of impressions, which was designed to anchor a reliable empirically based theory of knowledge, quickly translated into a collection of abstracted and decontexualized sense data, immediately given in a sensorial presence. Kant's critical rationalism continued to make purchases on the presence of abstracted transcendental conditions as basis for a theory of judgment. Although a classical metaphysics of presence is jettisoned in the epistemological turns of Hume and Kant, what is missing in their admittedly quite revolutionary philosophical contributions is a metaphysics to live by—a Dostoevskyian metaphysics that is palpitating with life as it lives through its manifold struggles with the frailities of finitude and the fractures of estrangment.

We have the good fortune to be able to select certain insights from Dostoevksy's "Underground Man" in our delineation of an ontology of human finitude that remains attentive to the clash of reason and passion in the travail of the life-experiencing subject. Dostoevsky is quick to acknowledge that reason is indeed a noble virtue, but it needs to be coupled with the passional side of human life in sketching a portrait of what it means to exist in a world that is often alien and threatening.[48] It is thus in the ruminations of the Underground Man that we find an early strategy of deconstruction with its attack on logocentrism. But this is a use of the ways of deconstruction to dismantle the absolute sovereignty of the rational side of human nature while being able to announce that it is still the case that "reason is an excellent thing." Clearly, the reason at issue here is a chastened and delimited reason, providing a sheet anchor against the absolutization of reason in the Great Crystal Palace as a symbol of the Enlightenment. But reason remains a vital resource, nonetheless, albeit operative within the limits of an ontology of human finitude. And as such it provides avenues for addressing the antireason proclivities in the postmodern challenge with its assaults on unity, presence, and identity.

A delimited notion of reason within a minimalist metaphysics allows one to recognize the realities of difference and multiplicity without succumbing to a knee-jerk rejection of identity and unity. Somewhat ironically, the representatives of radical postmodernity continue to make purchases on a mindset of dichotomization in which sameness (identity) and otherness (difference), unity and multiplicity, and homogeneity and heterogeneity are irrevocably pitted against each other, requiring a decision to opt for one or the other element in the polar opposition. Traveling with this dichotomous thinking, one can observe certain semantic vagaries in the vocabulary of postmodernity as it leaps from difference and multiplicity to paralogy and heterogeneity. It simply will not do to equate difference with paralogy and multiplicity with heterogeneity. The one does not slide into the other. Admittedly, we may be done with metanarratives of modernity that seek to reduce everything to undergirding unities and stable identities; but even our local narratives would fall short of communicability were it not for similarities among differences and continuities among multiplicities. The requirement that is placed before us is that of *splitting the difference* on matters of sameness versus difference and unity versus multiplicity.

Remaining attentive to the need to split the difference, one soon would be able to discern traces of an identity that does not solidify into a bedrock of incorrigible sameness. Delimited rationality makes it possible to revisit the past and project a future—both of which impinge on a present that is never that of a *pure* presence. Indeed it is a presence in the span of tension between a presence of brute factuality and an absence of fugitive nonbeing. The identity of the engaged subject within the confines of an ontology of human finitude is a mixture of presence and absence, being and nonbeing. Here one is at some distance from the abstracted and reified concept of identity as defined by relations of quantity and number. At issue is a vibrant notion of *personal* identity, an existential posture informed by a life of decision and commitment. It is the identity of self-knowledge and self-constitution that enables the self to be present to itself in both memory and hope, while exhibiting the fragility of a possible loss of selfhood. The achievement of personal identity is a continuing struggle against the dehumanization and depersonalization that is so poignantly illustrated in the life of Dostoevsky's Underground Man, who in his state of existential rebellion refuses to become a cog in a machine. It is precisely such a notion of personal identity that will play an important role in any future metaphysics that takes its point of departure from an ontology of human finitude.

Any elaboration and development of such a minimalist metaphysics proceeding from an ontology of human finitude will need to focus attention not only on the literary elucidations of the human condition by Dostoevsky but also on the existential insights of Søren

Kierkegaard. A recollection of the existential philosophy of Kierkegaard may well be the most urgent requirement of the times as we search for directions in fashioning the task of philosophy for the new millennium. It was Kierkegaard who effected his own deconstruction of the tiresome metaphysical speculations of both the ancients and the moderns. But he carried through this deconstruction in the interests of recovering the existential insights that informed the rise of metaphysics and were then lost in its serpentine history of speculative construction.

Such was particularly the case with his existential approach to the problem of self-identity and talk about the presence of the self. The issues at stake are approached not via the matrix of objectifying, abstract cosmological categories but rather via concrete descriptions and analyses of temporal existence. The criteria for self-identity are to be found in choice, decision, and action. One needs look for the meaning of identity not in abstract relations of number and quantity as they pertain to objects and things, but rather in the throes of choosing and deciding in our sojourns along life's way. We will then be able to observe the translation of self-identity and self-presence into *existential constancy* and *continuity*. This is what is to be learned by Judge William's instructions to the young aesthete in Kierkegaard's classic volume *Either/Or: A Fragment of Life:* "Even the richest personality is nothing before he has chosen himself, and on the other hand even what one might call the poorest personality is everything when he has chosen himself." And Judge William continues: "So the individual chooses himself as a concretion determined in manifold ways, and he chooses himself therefore in accord with his continuity."[49]

With Kierkegaard we are able to talk about self-identity in terms of an existential continuity that is achieved through the decisions and commitments that forge a constancy along the stages of life's way. In all this there are intimations of a "presence," albeit not the presence of a metaphysical monad or a putative selfsame object immune to the ravages of time. The presence at issue is that of an *existential* presence, embodied in time and space, wherewith the self is able to experiences its finite and fragile presence as that of being present to itself in its memory and in its hope. This is a presence that requires decision and commitment against the backdrop of recollection and anticipation. A self that has nothing to remember and nothing for which to hope is a self threatened by a loss of self-identity.

In our reflections on the future of metaphysics in response to the postmodern challenge, we have offered a sketch for a minimalist metaphysics, pruned of the heavy purchases on the resources of rationality and grandiose cosmological speculations on matters of being and nonbeing that are found in the tradition and are so baneful to the postmodern mind. We have expressed certain sympathies with the postmodernists' attacks on logocentrism and its heavy investment in metanarratives that espouse universal and unified world views. But we have stopped short of jettisoning metaphysical inquiry per se, and instead have suggested a reformulation of the task of metaphysics along the lines of an investigation of the being and behavior that we ourselves are, in our finite and temporal existence.

ESSAY V

The Task of Philosophy
for the New Millennium

IN NOVEMBER 1935 Edmund Husserl visited your city to present his famous Prague Lectures on "The Crisis of European Sciences and Psychology." This series of lectures subsequently became the basis of his much acclaimed later work, *The Crisis of European Sciences and Transcendental Phenomenology.* Because of an untimely death, he was unable to complete this work for publication. It was later published posthumously in 1954 under the editorship of Walter Biemel. Although the text of the projected volume remained an unfinished project, it has nonetheless become a work of immense philosophical importance.

It is now sixty-five years since the presentation of the *Crisis* in its skeletal form in Husserl's Prague Lectures. The central issue that is addressed in the later published volume is as relevant and as vibrant today as it was at the time that Husserl presented his Prague Lectures in 1935. The issue, then and now, has to do with the task and future of philosophy as an enterprise of reason. Husserl sets the guideline of his inquiry as follows:

> We are now certain that the rationalism of the eighteenth century, the manner in which it sought to secure the necessary roots of European humanity, was naive. But in giving up this naive and even absurd rationalism, is it necessary to sacrifice the *genuine* sense of rationalism? . . . The faith in the possibility of philosophy as a task,

that is, in the possibility of universal knowledge, is something we *cannot* let go. We *know* that we are *called* to this task as serious philosophers. And yet, how do we hold onto this belief, which has meaning only in relation to the single goal which is common to us all, that is, philosophy as such?[50]

What is the task that we are called to as serious philosophers? This is a question that needs to be taken up time and again—and always in the context of our historical situatedness. Our historical experience has brought us to an awareness of what Husserl called the naivité and indeed absurdity of the rationalism of the Age of Enlightenment, the rationalism that was designed to provide the foundations for the heavenly city of the eighteenth-century philosophers, the non-realization of which produced such a profound metaphysical disappointment. But should this lead us to a rejection of rationality in every sense conceivable? Husserl responds to this question with a resounding "no," and on this point we are in solid agreement with him.

In sketching the task of philosophy for the new millennium we will at times revisit Husserl's profound analysis of the crisis of European sciences, thinking with him as we map out new possibilities for the philosophy of the future. Our sketch will proceed along the lines of a tripartite format: (1) the naiveté of modern rationalism; (2) the postmodern voices of antireason; and (3) rationality as transversal.

The Naiveté of Modern Rationalism

Husserl's cultural critique of the European sciences pivots on his assessment of the rationalism of modernity as being naive. And by naiveté we are here to understand a complacent attitude and a taken-for-granted assumption that the objectifying procedures of scientific inquiry can provide us with the unassailable truths of our existence. The European sciences have developed an unrealistic faith in the resources of a *mathesis universalis,* and as a consequence they have lapsed into an objectivism that occludes the true origin of the sciences. Succumbing to the objectivating ideal of Galilean science as a universal method (which Husserl never confuses with the empirical procedures used by Galileo in conducting his experiments), both modern science and modern philosophy have lost their way in a labyrinth of formalization and quantification that conceals the region of the concrete lifeworld *(Lebenswelt)*, out of which all scientific experimentation and philosophical reflection arise. It is this universalization of the mathematical ideal that accounts for what Husserl names "the situational breakdown of our time" *(Zusammenbruchs-Situation unserer Zeit)*.

The proper response to this situational breakdown, avers Husserl, is a rigorous and radically reflective return to the lifeworld. The naiveté of modern rationalism within the sciences and philosophy alike has to do with their failure to recognize that human thought has its origins in a concrete lifeworld of perceptual, social, and praxis-oriented experience. It is the rich and variegated lifeworld that provides the sources for scientific and philosophical inquiry. This, however, does not mean that the quest for objectivity in the sciences and rationality in philosophy are to be abandoned. And it is particularly important to underscore the fact that the "crisis" that Husserl has in mind is *not* the result of the investigations and discoveries by Galileo, and much less the result of scientific inquiry as such. The principal target is the insidious *scientism* that has become manifest particularly in psychological behaviorism and philosophical positivism. And Husserl is equally adamant about not abandoning the resources of reason for the practice of philosophy. Indeed, the ideal of rationally based universal knowledge is an ideal Husserl says we cannot let go. But this ideal, continues Husserl, can be realized only when we lay hold of a *"genuine* sense of rationalism."

It is of some interest to point out that Husserl's cultural critique of the European sciences was linked with an internal critique of his own professional development, punctuating a distinction between the "early" and the "later" Husserl. It were as though Husserl came to realize that he had made too heavy purchases on the modern concept of reason in shaping his early program of "philosophy as a rigorous science." The project of philosophy as a rigorous science took as its guiding directive the maxim *Zu den Sachen selbst!* In the later project of the *Crisis* we find another guiding maxim, namely *Rückgang auf die Lebenswelt!* This staging of a return to the lifeworld is coupled with the admission that the earlier project of philosophy as a rigorous science is to be assessed as a dream from which one is now to be awakened. "Philosophy as science, as serious, rigorous, indeed apodictically rigorous, science—the *dream is over.*"[51]

Yet, one must proceed with some caution in interpreting this apparent reversal. This is not an announcement of an abandonment of rationality; nor is it a jettisoning of the transcendental requirement in philosophy. The second part of the title of this later work makes this point explicit—*The Crisis of European Sciences **and Transcendental Phenomenology***. So rationality and transcendental inquiry are not left behind. But surely they become significantly refigured in the move into Husserl's later thought. And for a commentary on this refiguration we have the rich philosophical legacy of Maurice Merleau-Ponty. With a firm grasp on Husserl's consummate contribution, Merleau-Ponty was able to consolidate the impact of Husserl's later period on the task of phenomenology for the future.

> Phenomenology is the study of essences, and according to it, all problems amount to finding definitions of essences: the essences of perception, or the essences of consciousness, for example. But phenomenology is also a philosophy which puts essences back into existence, and does not expect to arrive at an understanding of man and the world from any starting point other than that of their "facticity." It is a transcendental philosophy which places in abeyance the assertions arising out of the natural attitude, the better to understand them; but it is also a philosophy for which the world is always "already there" before reflection begins—as an inalienable presence—and all its efforts are concentrated upon achieving a direct and primitive contact with the world, and endowing that contact with a philosophical status. It is the search for a philosophy which shall be a "rigorous science," but it also offers an account of space, time and the world as we "live" them.[52]

In expanding and consolidating the main features of the naiveté of modern rationalism, it is necessary to explicate the epistemological and ontological commitments that inform its agendum. And here one is able to appropriate insights from both Husserl and Merleau-Ponty. Plainly enough, the appetition for a *mathesis universalis* on the part of modernity led to an ontologization of the scientific method as the universal logos that is to guide all inquiry. This became particularly evident in the development of positivism, which illustrated its own species of metaphysics in spite of its alleged antimetaphysical posture. The philosopher of a positvistic frame of mind readily consents to the truth *in the beginning was the logos,* but he is adamant that the logos that was from the very beginning is a universal structure of meaning that has only two features—logical self-evidence and empirical verifiability. In this accentuated restriction of the range of meaning in the positivists' criteria for demonstrable knowledge, the forms of perception and the strategies of understanding for a reclamation of a direct contact with the life-world were effectively occluded. In viewing rationality as identical to the formalism of logic and the quantification procedures of scientific validation, positivism succumbed to an objectivist ideology that concealed the origins of science and philosophy alike.

The stage for the nineteenth- and twentieth-century positivistic reductionism, however, had already been set by earlier epistemological proclivities of modernity. And here the father of modern philosophy, René Descartes, does not remain entirely faultless. In effecting the epistemological turn of modernity, Descartes bears the responsibility for a criteriologically based theory of knowledge in which the criteria for reliable knowledge need to be front loaded, determined in advance via a delineation of methodological rules of procedure. Descartes's "Rules of Method," which find their touchstone in the mathematical sciences, provide a clear illustration of a rule-governed approach to philosophical truth that is governed by the ideal of a *mathesis universalis.* The rule of certainty, which leads the pack, specifies clear and distinct ideas as the tribunal before which all epistemological claims need to be justified. The method for attaining knowledge, with its accompanying criteria for truth, are laid out in advance in an axiomatic format. This format prescribes rule-governed procedures of deduction and inference, designed to deliver apodictic (universal and necessary) knowledge. Only then will the rule of certainty have delivered its goods.

This valorization of method, predelineated criteria, rule-governed procedures, and the ideal of apodicticity, all congealed into the grand hypothesis of the modern logos, in which the ancient *logos* became analyzed into the modern *epistēmē,* and theory was elevated to a status of preeminence as practice became subordinated to at best an "application" of theory. The logos of modern rationalism was announced in a celebration of *epistēmē* at the expense of *doxa.* The epistemological turn in the search of the *logos* of the *epistēmē* became the defining mark of modernity. It is surely this disparagment of *doxa,* what Husserl calls "the disdainful coloring of the *doxa*" *(die verächtliche Färbung der doxa),* that provides much of the background in Husserl's critique of modern rationalism.[53] It is precisely through a reclamation of the resources of *doxa,* with its "functioning intentionality" *(fungierende Intentionalität),* that the return to the lifeworld is to be accomplished. There is an intentionality, an upsurge of meaning, that is older than pure theory, and which is operative in the concretely lived-through experiences of everyday life. There is an insight and understanding ensconced in our quotidian praxis-oriented existence that modern rationalism has glossed. To be sure, the pursuit of knowledge as a genuine epistemic adventure remains the task and goal of philosophy, but when philosophy loses its mooring in the rarified heights of pure theory the concrete lifeworld is destined for displacement and the crisis of the European sciences remains in force.

The naiveté of modern rationalism was illustrated not only in the areas of epistemology and metaphysics but also in the domain of social and political philosophy. Reason was considered by the Enlightenment thinkers as that trustworthy torch that could lead us to a rational social order, possessing the proper ingredients of a pharmakon for treating the ills of modern society. A profound optimism with regard to the resources of science and technology provided modern rationalism with a pronounced technocratic expression. With the proper implementation of control mechanisms and predictive devices it was believed that the future could be shaped to fit our ideals of a perfect society. Rationality, predictability, perfectibility, and progressivism were linked in such a way that they virtually became convertible terms.

The manifestation of modern rationalism in its socio-political guise assumed the shape of a quite aggressive *historicism.* This was an historicism informed by a distinctive stance on the nature of historical time as a linear development proceeding to a realization of utopian ideals. These utopian ideals congealed into what Carl Becker suggestively named "the heavenly city of the eighteenth-century philosophers" in his witty and ironic book by that name.[54] That which informed the utopianism of modern historicism was its peculiar take on the three dimensions of historical time. The past was viewed as a reservoir of historical facts, which could be known through the objective procedures of the scientific method. Science and technology, it was believed, had brought us to the stage of development in which we could know the past as it actually happened. The attitude toward the present in historicism was one of a facile relativism in which no moral claims assumed an obliging character. The attitude toward the future was anchored in an overt optimism fueled by notions of human perfectibility and indefinite progress. The factors that led to the problematization and eventual breakup of historicism were both philosophical and socio-political in nature. Nietzsche in his essay "The Use and Abuse of History" harpooned the pretensions of an historicism bent upon achieving scientifically based and objective knowledge of the past. Twentieth-century existentialism, with its key notions of involvement *(engagé)*, commitment, and uncertainty, countered the historicists' claims for a theoretically detached knowledge of the past; its uncommitted ethical stance on the demands of the present; and its illusions of a predictable future. The socio-political events of the twentieth century offered their own indictment of the vagaries of the historicist doctrines of human perfectibility and inevitable progress. A global economic depression, two world wars that brought into question the future of the modern nation state, and unthinkable experiments in politically motivated programs of genocide, provided testimony of a profound metaphysical disappointment that followed in the wake of the naive rationalism of modern historicism.

THE POSTMODERN VOICES OF ANTIREASON

Traveling with Husserl for a significant stretch of the road, we define the philosophical task for the new millennium as being that of a recovery of a "genuine" rationality after the resources of modern rationalism and historicism have become impoverished. But as we travel this road we encounter another obstacle that presents us with a formidable challenge—the advent of postmodernism and its antireason posture. This antireason posture is basically a fallout from the postmodern assault on *logocentrism*. Although given different expressions by members of the postmodern camp, logocentrism is understood to encompass a sizeable chunk of philosophical history from the ancients through the modern period. It is defined as the mindset that extolls the virtues of human reason; searches for apodictic foundations of epistemology; offers metaphysical claims for universality, totality, and identity; makes claims for absolutes in ethics; and imputes a progressivistic teleology to history. On all of these accounts, postmodern thinkers are of the mind that trafficers in logocentrism come up short and that it is time to declare the logos itself as bankrupt. In its state of reaction, postmodernity rejects foundationalist claims for epistemological grounding; celebrates particularity, multiplicity, and difference; settles for the relativity of ethical and political norms; and abjures the grammar of *arche* and *telos* in discourses about history. It is thus that the postmodern assault on logocentrism does indeed appear very much to congeal into a posture of *anti*-reason.

An interesting and rather paradoxical set of relationships emerges in a comparison of Husserl's critique of the naive rationalism of modernity and the voices of antireason in postmodernity. It would appear that postmodernists are in agreement with Husserl in his critical assessment of modern rationalism. He renounced the doctrine of the logos in the guise of a *mathesis universalis* and he rescued the trammeled doxa from a fate of objectivization. This surely ought elicit applause from the postmodernist camp. However, Husserl was not ready to jettison the logos in every sense you please. Indeed, it is a revised and revitalized logos, in the guise of a "genuine rationalism," that is called upon to guide us toward the goal of the philosophy of the future. Hence, the logos as a principle of rationality is not to be abandoned. It is to be properly viewed as a resource for penetrating the doxastic beliefs and practices that stimulate the economy of the lifeworld. But it is precisely this resource of rationality that is placed into question by postmodernism. And instead of the "despised doxa" of modernity we are confronted with the "despised logos" of postmodernity.

Various postmodern voices have converged in the disparagement of the logos as resource of reason in the everyday life of civil society. The voice of Jean-François Lyotard may be the most explicit. "There is no politics of reason," he writes, "neither in the sense of a totalizing reason nor in that of the concept. And so we must do with a politics of opinion."[55] Our situation is such, according to Lyotard, that our only resources reside in a politics of opinion (doxa) instead of a politics of reason (logos). Lyotard's consummate characterization of postmodernism has become a password for all initiates in the movement. Postmodernism, says Lyotard, boils down to "incredulity toward metanarratives," a "sensitivity to differences," a "tolerating of the incommensurable," "living with the inventor's paralogy," and waging "a war on totality."[56] This pretty much sums up matters as regards the postmodern posture.

Although postmodernism has not congealed into anything that approximates a unified doctrinal program, there are the well-known contributors to its loosely defined mindset referenced in philosophical circles. It is also common knowledge that postmodernism is practiced in cognate fields—such as architecture, the fine arts, literary studies, political theory, the social sciences, and theology. This all makes a definition of the movement more difficult. However, even in these cognate areas, a dissatisfaction with requirements and norms of rationality becomes readily apparent. In the discipline of philosophy, which itself has no unified grammar and format, the names commonly associated with postmodern thought include Nietzsche as forerunner and Heidegger as early founder. Jacques Derrida's project of a radical deconstruction of the metaphysics of presence, both ancient and modern, merits an entry in the lexicon of postmodernism as an illustration of left-wing Heideggerianism. Also, commonly referenced as representatives of postmodernism are Gilles Deleuze and Félix Guattari with their root metaphor of "the rhizomatic" (as contrasted with "the arborescent"), which portrays reality as a perpetual and evanescent becoming, constantly subject to differentiation and pluralization, sans *arche* and *telos,* without either origin or end. Michel Foucault is often included in the group—and this in spite of the fact that in one of his later interviews he denied knowing what "postmodernism" might mean! Nonetheless, his genealogical method and his preoccupation with an analysis of the network of power relations within local and micropractices are quite consistent with the postmodern devaluation of a totalizing rationality.

There are of course other putative representatives of the postmodern persuasion in philosophy. Julia Kristeva and Luce Irigaray have multidisciplinary backgrounds in philosophy, psychology, and literary theory and have elicited increasing interest across the disciplines both in their native Europe and in North America. Particularly noteworthy in the philosophical contribution coming from the United States is the work of Richard Rorty. His book *Philosophy and the Mirror of Nature* appeared on the scene as a veritable literary bombshell, exploding numerous caches of philosophical claims in analytical philosophy, of which he was a previous adherent.[57] Singling out Dewey, Heidegger, and Wittgenstein as his heroes, Rorty carries through a radical refiguration of the terrain of philosophy. One could well speak of this as the American version of postmodernity. Rorty will have no truck with philosophical metanarratives. Philosophy can no longer pretend to speak for eternity. It is no more than a local voice in the conversation of humankind in which it is incumbent upon the interlocutors to remain with that which language permits one to say. Clearly, the logocentrism of the classical tradition falls under indictment, but Rorty also remains critical of Husserl's revisionary rationalism, as well as of Habermas's communicatively based reason. They are still caught up, Rorty argues, in the criteriological paradigm of modern epistemology, seeking to provide a rational reconstruction of knowledge after the supports of epistemology as a curious theory of knowledge about knowledge have been called into question.

So where does this all leave the task of philosophy for the new millennium? There may indeed be a question as to whether philosophy has a future task at all in the aftermath of such a vigorous postmodern assault! Admittedly, one may need to remain highly skeptical about the future of philosophy as a quest for a rational unification of experience based on a view from eternity, but there surely will continue to be conversations about what one can believe, what one ought to do, and for what one might hope. However, postmodernists want us to face up to the reality that there can be no obliging rational sanctions for our discourse and action on these and other matters. The problem within the philosophical economy, they insist, is that its investments in the unifying power of reason have ended up in the red, and this is because the investments were ill-fated from the outset.

Those of us who still hold out for a future for philosophy and its telos of reason have a responsibility to address the challenge of postmodernism. And this involves achieving as much clarity as possible on what the fuss about matters of rationality is all about. In addressing this challenge, which is veritably a formidable one, it might be that there are some insights, critiques, and proposals by the proponents of postmodernity that need to be heeded and in some cases possibly appropriated.

The postmodern challenge as regards the role of reason very much turns on the issues of universality versus particularity, identity versus difference, and unity versus multiplicity. Universality, identity, and unity have pretty much called the shots in the ancient metaphysical and the modern epistemological doctrines of the logos. The logos is at once identical with itself and unifies everything else, gathering the whole of reality under its purview, managing particularity through the measure of universality. And this is precisely the logocentrism that postmoderns find to be so problematic. To be sure, it is not the case that the range of reason has remained uncontested in the modern period. Indeed, it was Kant's singular contribution to delimit the reach of rationality in the philosophical quest. Given the ineradicable finitude of human reason, Kant was driven to the conclusion that knowledge of ultimate reality remains unattainable. Knowledge of the human soul, the cosmos, and God is at best regulative but never constitutive. In the moment that these "Ideas of Reason" are employed in the service of constitutive knowledge, seeking a unification of both the subjective and objective conditions of experience, the end result is a paralogism (a formal fallacy of four terms) in the argument for an immaterial soul, antinomies in an attempted demonstration that the cosmos is either finite or infinite, and a transcendental illusion that results from a misapplication of the categories of existence and causality in an effort to demonstrate the existence of a supernatural being.

Yet, Kant was not ready to jettison the grammars of apodicticity, universality, necessity, unity, and identity, and it is these grammars that postmodernists find to be so offensive. Admittedly, in Kant's critical rationalism these grammars were shorn of their metaphysical capital. But they were assigned new roles to play in the adventure of epistemological grounding. The invention of the transcendental unity of apperception, which may have been Kant's greatest achievement, is illustrative of the continuing quest for a rational reconstruction of knowledge wherewith to found claims for universality and necessity. For the postmodernist these claims for universality and necessity become misplaced preoccupations with problems that are the result of scratching where it does not itch. They are quite removed from the discourses and actions that define the particularities, contingencies, and multiplicities of our everyday social practices.

The challenge of postmodernism to come to terms with these particularities, contingencies, and multiplicities—and with the *differance* that is alleged to pervade them all—is indeed a challenge that merits a response. As the telos of Kant's project was "to save the appearances," so an appropriate response to the postmodern challenge would need to be designed as an effort to save the integrity of *differance* as a multifaceted alterity that plays itself out in the economy of our diversified discursive and social practices. But we need to experiment with doing the saving without an appeal to either transcendental or empirical reconstructions of knowledge. Such an appeal is veritably a dream of modernity that has run its course. This does not mean, however, that our perception, our discourse, and our action—all of which make up the fabric of our communicative praxis—are therefore bereft of rationality. Clearly, in our perceptions and in our discourses and in our actions an understanding and an explanation of our being-in-the-world is set forth, and this is an understanding and explanation that does not need to wait on a foundationalist justification of knowledge, whether in a transcendental or empirical guise. We need to find a space for rationality between the abstracted polar elements that comprise what Foucault has piquantly named "the empirico-transcendental doublet." We have come to call this rationality between the sequestered particularities of modern empiricism (bare facts, raw impressions, sense data, etc.) and the transcendentally determined universals of modern rationalism (apriori truth conditions) by the name of *transversal rationality*. The transversal logos replaces the universal logos as the lynch-pin for the philosophy of the new millennium.

RATIONALITY AS TRANSVERSAL

The thesis that we wish to proffer is that the crisis of the European sciences that Husserl addressed, and the more recent encompassing crisis occasioned by an increasing globalization of world society as we move into the new millennium, can be most productively engaged through an appeal to the resources of a transversal rationality. The concept of transversality, admittedly, is not of recent date. It has already done duty in the fields of mathematics, nuclear physics, physiology, and anatomy. Mathematicians working in the specialized area of topology have used the concept in their explorations of geometrical space, in which transversality functions as a generalization of orthoganility explaining the convergence of lines and surfaces without coincidence. Physicists have employed the concept in their investigations of physical space, defining the ratio of accelerating forces in terms of transverse mass. Physiologists speak of the transversality of entwined fibres, and anatomists use the concept to explain the dynamic functioning of vertebrae.

The concept has also been called upon to perform a function for the philosophical sciences, and here one is of course immediately reminded of Jean-Paul Sartre's use of the term to account for the peculiar unity of consciousness in his classic work *The Transcendence of the Ego*. It is in this work that he defines consciousness, understood against the backdrop of Husserl's doctrine of intentionality, as that "which unifies itself, concretely, by a play of 'transversal' intentionalities which are concrete and real retentions of past consciousness."[58] Sartre's use of the term, however, still remains quite restrictive, given his philosophical prejudice for proceeding from the primacy of a sovereign consciousness, with the consequence that a wider application and use of the concept remains effectively blocked. What is required is an exploration of the efficacy of the concept within the wider polis of our communicative practices. The dynamics of a transversal rationality and communication structures our amalgamated discourse and action as it informs social practices, institutional organizations, and our wider politico-cultural existence. The recognition of this wider matrix of transversality becomes a particular urgency as one moves into an accelerating globalization that may well become the defining mark of the new millennium.

Convergence without coincidence, unification without equivalence, commonality without identity, assimilation without absorption, and cooperation without uniformity—these interrelated senses define the texture and dynamics of transversality. Clearly at work in this interplay of senses is the ingression of *differance* and the requirement for a full recognition of the role of alterity. Transversality highlights the integrity of otherness without, however, installing it as a first principle. Neither sameness nor otherness, neither identity nor difference, are first principles, vying for a subordination of the one to the other. And it is precisely transversality that provides a sheet anchor against such a subordination. Its economy is situated between the economy of a universalizing rationality with its heavy purchases on a metaphysics and epistemology of identity/sameness and the economy of an antireason with its rhapsody of unbounded difference/otherness.

This concept of transversality, which has served us so well in the mathematical, physical, and life sciences, now needs to be explicated, interpreted, and expanded vis-a-vis its relevance for the present task of philosophy that calls us to address the crises of our ethical and cultural existence as we move into a new century and a new millennium. Confronted with a plurality of social practices, a heterogeneity of political ideologies, and a plethora of religious differences, the ethical requirement becomes that of discerning the fitting response to the myriad discourses and actions that invade the wider polis. There are conflicts both theoretical and concretely political that divide Israelies and Palestinians, Muslims and Hindus, Serbs and Croats, the Irish Republic and the British Crown. These are examples of what Lyotard has suggestively named the *differend,* a conflict between two parties that cannot be equitably resolved for lack of a rule of judgment applicable to both sides of the controversy.[59] What are the resources of rationality for dealing with such situations of global crises? Is there a strategy that might enable one to move to an understanding, or even agreement if only in a provisional way, while acknowledging the integrity of the parties in dispute and the legitimacy of the claims in conflict?

The rationality that is able to meet the challenges of the philosophy of the future is a rationality transversally textured, oriented toward a transversal communication that is able to move across the landscape of differences, striving for agreements and cooperative ventures *in spite of* differences, realizing that a multiplicity of perspectives is not ipso facto a deterrent to shared concerns and goals but can indeed be a source of mutual enrichment. Convergence without coincidence—such is the directive of transversal rationality. To agree on a workable plan of action one need not achieve a coincidence of beliefs. But to proceed within such a framework one needs to suspend, if not indeed abandon, the quest for certainty on matters of beliefs and principles that yearn for a foundationalism that is anchored in claims for unimpeachable universality and necessity. Rorty's advice to be done with the vagaries of foundationalism should be taken to heart. But to be done with foundationalism as a rational reconstruction of knowledge is not to be done with either reason or knowledge in every sense conceivable. Rather it issues a call to the hard struggle of transversal communication informed by a rationality that forges a passage between the Scylla of a universal logos and the Charybdis of a facile abandonment of the logos. And it is in heeding this call that we are able to split the difference as it were between the universal and the particular, the necessary and the contingent, the one and the many, the solidarity of consensus and the agonistics of dissensus. The dream of a unity of the sciences grounded in a *mathesis universalis* will need to be asssessed along the lines of the critique by the later Husserl as a dream that has run its course. But also we will need to come to a realization that the anarchic particularity of an antilogos doctrine contains the seeds of its own destruction.

How does this directive for transversal rationality and transversal communication play itself out in the lifeworld of our concrete social practices and institutional formations of our cultural existence? Ultimately one needs to search out illustrations of the workings of transversality in particular cases. A helpful illustration of such has been provided by the French psychiatrist Félix Guattari in his description of the dynamics at work in what he calls "transversality in the group."[60] The specific group that he analyzes as an exemplification of the dynamics of transversality is the constitutive network that makes up the operation of a psychiatric practice. The institutional setting for the practice of psychiatry is made up of a network of involved parties, including the administrators of the hospital, the doctors, the nurses, assistants to the doctors and the nurses, patients, the families of the patients, and the friends of the patients. These are the groups and the subgroups that comprise the institutional setting of the psychiatric practice, and all of these groups play some role in the healing process. They all have, if you will, a voice in the decision making and the determination of strategies and procedures. But for this decision making to be effective, according to Guattari, it needs to be transversal to the different groups and the various social roles that make up the institutional complex.

There are multiple rationales at work, issuing from the different groups and subgroups. And transversality is achieved when there is an effective dialogue across the various groups with their distinctive rationales. This requires, of course, a recognition of the integrity of the "otherness" of each of the parties involved. The net result is a heightened understanding by each of the involved parties and a mutual acknowledgment of certain adjustments and accommodations that need to be made to maximize the results of the healing process. Guattari refers to this as a process of "dialectical enrichment."

The principal point at issue is that, in developing self-understanding and encouraging cooperative ventures in the sundry establishments of institutional management in our civil society, it is a transversal dialectic that enables one to avoid both the hegemony of a decision-making process that proceeds vertically from top down and the stalemate of horizontally dispersed groups warring with each other. Guattari pointedly summarizes the requirement for the transversal matrix in achieving maximal social equilibrium when he writes: "Transversality is a dimension that tries to overcome the impasse of pure verticality and that of mere horizontality; it tends to be achieved when there is a maximum communication among the different levels, and above all, in different meanings."[61]

We submit, in conclusion, that an unavoidable task of philosophy for the new millennium is that of installing the dynamics of transversal rationality and transversal communication across the landscape of differences within an increasingly global and pluralistic world order. Only this will save us from the impasse created by the collision of a hegemony of universally legislated belief systems and policies with a rampant relativism of chaotic particularity and multiplicity. The world of tomorrow will be a world in which we no longer will be able to view national, ethnic, political, ethical, and religious differences from afar. As a result of increasing globalization these differences of beliefs and practices are bought to our thresholds, and we are confronted with the demand to work out policies and procedures of how to deal with our personal and social identities among differences.

We are fortunate to have assistance in this formidable task in the person and writings of Martin J. Matuštík, whose name it is peculiarly appropriate to invoke in my current discussions with you. Professor Matuštík is a former Czeck national and student signatory of the *Charta 77 Manifesto*. In his 1993 work, *Postnational Identity,* he develops a strategy for thinking beyond the ideological conflicts of capitalism and communism, as well as related conflicting ethnic and religious perspectives, by sketching a basis for establishing an entwined political and self-identity against the backdrop of Habermas's critical social theory and the existential reflections in the thought of Søren Kierkegaard and Vaclav Havel. Combining the rationality of critical social theory with existential pathos and reflection, Matuštík makes a case for a postnational identity that remains respondent to the multicultural realities of the lifeword, as he furrows a path to a participatory democracy that moves between the universalism of a hegemony-based consensus and a capitulation to unmanageable particularism and dissensus.[62]

As we move into the new millennium we will no longer have the luxury of dealing with ethnic, religious, and political differences with doctrinal certitude, appealing to our own beliefs and practices as universally valid. We will need to communicate with that which is other, different, and alien. This communication with the varied expressions of alterity requires a self- and cultural transcendence whereby one acknowledges the integrity of that which is other, striving for communication *in spite of* the differences, always seeking convergence without coincidence. When this occurs we will have achieved, even if only momentarily, the posture of a transversal rationality that will enable each one of us to acknowledge each other as inhabitants of a common earth. And in doing so we will have responded to Husserl's charge to strive for "a *genuine* sense of rationalism."

NOTES

1. Richard Rorty, *Philosophy and the Mirror of Nature* (Princeton: Princeton University Press, 1979). See particularly chapter four, "Privileged Representations," pp. 165–212.

2. For the author's elaboration of communicative praxis as an amalgam of discourse and action, anterior to both metaphysical construction and epistemological criteriology, see his book *Communicative Praxis and the Space of Subjectivity* (West Lafayette: Purdue University Press, 2003).

3. David Hume, *A Treatise of Human Nature,* ed. L. A. Selby-Bigge (Oxford: Clarendon, 1888), p. 253.

4. See particularly Jacques Derrida, *Speech and Phenomena and Other Essays on Husserl's Theory of Signs,* trans. David B. Allison (Evanston: Northwestern University Press, 1973).

5. See Edmund Husserl, *The Crisis of European Sciences and Transcendental Phenomenology,* trans. David Carr (Evanston: Northwestern University Press, 1970).

6. See particularly Mikhail M. Bakhtin, *The Dialogic Imagination,* trans. Caryl Emerson and Michael Holquist (Austin: University of Texas Press, 1981).

7. Paul Ricoeur, *Time and Narrative,* vols. 1 & 2, trans. Kathleen McLaughlin and David Pellauer; vol. 3, trans. Kathleen Blamey and David Pellauer (Chicago: University of Chicago Press, 1958–88).

8. Stanley Cavell, *The Claim of Reason: Wittgenstein, Skepticism, Morality, and Tragedy* (Oxford: Oxford University Press. 1979), p. 8. In this connection see also John Wild, "Is There a World of Ordinary Language?" *Philosophical Review,* 68 (October, 1958), 460–76.

9. See particularly "Introduction: Traditional Prejudices and the Return to Phenomena" in *Phenomenology of Perception,* trans. Colin Smith (New York: Humanities, 1962).

10. Here we need to be reminded of Søren Kierkegaard's role in the deconstruction of the Greek concept of recollection as it stood in the service of metaphysical interests. See his book *Repetition: An Essay in Experimental Psychology,* trans. Walter Lowrie (Princeton: Princeton University Press, 1946), and particularly page 3–4: "*Repetition* is a decisive expression for what "recollection" was for the Greeks. Just as they taught that all knowledge is a recollection, so will modern philosophy teach that the whole of life is repetition. The only modern philosopher who had an inkling of this was Leibniz. Repetition and recollection are the same movement, only in opposite directions; for what is recollected has been, is repeated backward, whereas repetition properly so called is recollected forwards.

11. Jacques Derrida, *Of Grammatology,* trans. Gayatri Spivak (Baltimore: Johns Hopkins University Press, 1974), p. 158.

12. Paul Ricoeur, *Time and Narrative,* vol. 3, p. 261.

13. Michel Foucault, *The Order of Things: An Archaeology of the Human Sciences* (New York: Random House, 1970), p. 387.

14. Martin Heidegger, *The Basic Problems of Phenomenology,* trans. Albert Hofstadter (Bloomington: Indiana University Press, 1982), p. 23.

15. Richard Macksey and Eugenio Donato, eds., *The Languages of Criticism and the Sciences of Man: The Structuralist Controversy* (Baltimore: Johns Hopkins University Press, 1970), p. 271.

16. Jacques Derrida, *Of Grammatology,* trans. Gayatri Spivak (Baltimore: Johns Hopkins University Press, 1974), p. 158.

17. Gilbert Ryle, *The Concept of Mind* (New York: Barnes and Noble, 1949), pp. 11–12.

18. In *Mind: A Quarterly Review of Psychology and Philosophy,* vol. 38, 1929, p. 370.

19. See particularly Gabriel Marcel, *Etre et avoir* (Fernand Aubier: Editions Montaigne, 1935) and *The Mystery of Being,* vol. I, trans. G. S. Fraser (Chicago: Henry Regnery, 1960). Also see Maurice Merleau-Ponty, *Phe-*

nomenology of Perception, trans. Colin Smith (New York: Humanities, 1962), and especially "Part One: The Body," pp. 67–199.

20. Émile Benveniste, *Problems in General Linguistics,* trans. Mary Elizabeth Beek (Coral Gables: University of Miami Press, 1971), p. 224.

21. Maurice Merleau-Ponty, *Phenomenology of Perception,* p. 426.

22. Paul Ricoeur, *Freedom and Nature: The Voluntary and the Involuntary,* trans. Erazim Kohák (Evanston: Northwestern University Press, 1966), p. 58.

23. Michel Foucault, "Truth and Power," in *Power/Knowledge,* Colin Gordan, ed. (New York: Pantheon, 1980), p. 117.

24. William James, *Essays in Radical Empiricism* (New York: Longmans, Green, 1942), p. 170n.

25. See particularly Edmund Husserl, *Logische Untersuchungen,* vol. 2 (Halle: Max Niemeyer, 1913), p. 208. See also Husserl's essay *"Persönliche Aufzeichungen,"* in *Philosophy and Phenomenological Research,* 16 (1956), p. 295.

26. For a comprehensive discussion of the lines of relationship between James's radical empiricism and phenomenology see Bruce Wilshire, *William James and Phenomenology* (Bloomington: Indiana University Press, 1968). In his book Wilshire argues for the emergence of an indigenous American phenomenology in the philosophy of James. To be sure, he recognizes common topics and themes and even possible mutual influence issuing from both sides of the Atlantic. But American phenomenology is seen as having an *elan* of its own, not dependent on some of the longstanding metaphysical and epistemological ruminations that can still be found in the Continental tradition.

27. Herbert Spiegelberg, *The Phenomenological Movement,* 2 (The Hague, 1960), p. 563.

28. Paul Ricoeur, *Husserl: An Analysis of His Phenomenology* (Evanston: Northwestern University Press, 1967), pp. 213–33.

29. Paul Ricoeur, *Freedom and Nature: The Voluntary and the Involuntary,* trans. Erazim Kohák (Evanston: Northwestern University Press, 1966), p. 58.

30. Paul Ricoeur, *Oneself as Another,* trans. Kathleen Blamey (Chicago: University of Chicago Press, 1992), p. 57.

31. See Calvin O. Schrag, *Communicative Praxis and the Space of Subjectivity* (West Lafayette: Purdue University Press, 2003), and particularly chapter 6, "Hermeneutical Self-implicature," pp.115–38.

32. *The Languages of Criticism and the Sciences of Man,* ed. Richard Macksey and Eugenio Donato (Baltimore: Johns Hopkins Press, 1970), p. 271.

33. *Who Comes after the Subject?* ed. Eduardo Cadava, Peter Connor, and Jean-Luc Nancy (New York: Routledge, 1991), p. 100.

34. Jacques Derrida, *Edmund Husserl's **Origin of Geometry:** An Introduction,* translated, with a preface , by John P. Leavey, Jr.; David B. Allison, ed. (Stony Brook, N.Y.: Nicolas Hays, 1976), p. 29.

35. Emmanuel Levinas, *Of God Who Comes to Mind,* trans. Bettina Bergo (Stanford: Stanford University Press, 1998), p. 26.

36. *Of God Who Comes to Mind,* p. 26.

37. See particularly chapter 10, "Ethos, Ethics, and a New Humanism," in *Communicative Praxis and the Space of Subjectivity,* pp. 197–214.

38. *Letters of Fyodor Michailovitch Dostoevsky to His Family and Friends,* trans. Ethel Colburn Mayne (New York: Horizon, 1961), p. 67.

39. Nicholas Berdyaev, *Dostoevsky,* trans. Donald Attwater (New York: Meridian, 1957), p. 11.

40. André Gide, *Dostoevsky* (Connecticut: New Directions, 1961), p. 16.

41. Quoted in Walter Kaufmann, *Nietzsche: Philosopher, Psychologist, Antichrist* (New York: Random House, 1968), p. 340.

42. Emmanuel Levinas, *Outside the Subject,* trans. Michael B. Smith (Stanford: Stanford University Press, 1994), p. 44.

43. Hans-Georg Gadamer, *Reason in the Age of Science,* trans. Frederick G. Lawrence (Cambridge, Mass.: MIT, 1981), p. 81.

44. Jean-François Lyotard, *The Postmodern Condition: A Report on Knowledge,* trans. Geoff Bennington and Brian Massumi (Minneapolis: University of Minnesota Press, 1984), p. xxiv–xxv.

45. Jacques Derrida, *Speech and Phenomena and other Essays on Husserl's Theory of Signs,* trans. David B. Allison and Newton Garver (Evanston: Northwestern University Press, 1973), pp. 147, 159.

46. See particularly Jacques Derrida, "White Mythology: Metaphor in the Text of Philosophy" in *Margins of Philosophy,* trans. Alan Bass (Chicago: University of Chicago Press, 1982).

47. Jacques Derrida, *Speech and Phenomena and other Essays on Husserl's Theory of Signs,* trans. David B. Allison (Evanston: Northwestern University Press, 1973). See particularly chapter 4, "Meaning and Representation," pp. 48–59.

48. "You see, gentlemen, reason is an excellent thing, there's no disputing that, but reason is nothing but reason and satisfies only the rational side of man's nature, while will is a manifestation of the whole life, that is, of the whole human life including reason and all the impulses," *Notes from Underground* in Walter Kaufmann, *Existentialism from Dostoevsky to Sartre* (New York: Meridian, 1956), p. 73.

49. Søren Kierkegaard, *Either/Or: A Fragment of Life,* vol. 2, trans. David F. Swenson and Lillian M. Swenson (Princeton: Princeton University Press, 1949), pp. 150, 211.

50. Edmund Husserl, *The Crisis of European Sciences and Transcendental Phenomenology,* trans. David Carr (Evanston: Northwestern University Press, 1970), pp. 16, 17.

51. *The Crisis,* p. 389.

52. Maurice Merleau-Ponty, *Phenomenology of Perception,* trans. Colin Smith (New York: Humanities, 1962), p. vii.

53. *The Crisis,* p. 125.

54. Carl L. Becker, *The Heavenly City of the Eighteenth-Century Philosophers* (New Haven: Yale University Press, 1932).

55. Jean-François Lyotard and Jean-Loup Thébaud, *Just Gaming,* trans. Wlad Godzich (Minneapolis: University of Minnesota Press, 1985), p. 82.

56. Jean-François Lyotard, *The Postmodern Condition: A Report on Knowledge,* trans. Geoff Bennington and Brian Massumi (Minneapolis: University of Minnesota Press, 1984), pp. xxiv, xxv, 82.

57. Richard Rorty, *Philosophy and the Mirror of Nature* (Princeton: Princeton University Press, 1979).

58. Jean-Paul Sartre, *The Transcendence of the Ego: An Existential Theory of Consciousness,* trans. Forrest Williams and Robert Kirkpatrick (New York: Noonday, 1957), p. 39.

59. See particularly Jean-François Lyotard, *The Differend: Phrases in Dispute,* trans. Georges Van Den Abbeele (Minneapolis: University of Minnesota Press, 1988).

60. Félix Guattari, *Molecular Revolution: Psychiatry and Politics,* trans. Rosemary Sheed (New York: Penguin, 1984), p. 22.

61. *Molecular Revolution,* p. 18.

62. Martin J. Matuštík, *Postnational Identity: Critical Theory and Existential Philosophy in Habermas, Kierkegaard, and Havel* (New York: Guilford, 1993).

NAME INDEX